Karen:

Keep breaking the evil spell of sameness every day.

Cheers
Tim Wunilson

UNCOMMODiFiED

a Provocative & Practical Guide
to **STANDiNG UP & STANDiNG OUT** in a Crowded World

BEING WRITTEN BY:
Tim Windsor & Maybe You

The Legal Stuff - UNCOMMODiFiED STYLE

All rights to these words, ideas, musings, rants, and any other stuff in here are reserved. No part of this publication may be reproduced, stored or transmitted in any form or by any means, electronic, mechanical, photocopying (do people still do this?), recording, scanning, transmitting to aliens in another galaxy or here on earth, communicated to very smart monkeys and or any other sea, land, or sky creature, or in any other crazy ass way you can think of to rip off all this hard work without written permission from the publisher or author. And it really is illegal (and you may go to jail forever or be flogged publicly on social media) if you copy this book, post it to a website, attach the pages to carrier pigeons, or distribute it by any other means known to humanity without permission. And be also warned that if you do any of these things, my mom may come back from the grave to bitch slap you and possibly haunt you forever and ever and ever ... and that's a very long time.

Tim Windsor assumes zero, nada, zilch, no responsibility for the persistence or accuracy of external or third-party Internet Websites referred to in this publication. Additionally, he does not guarantee that any content on such Websites is, or will remain, accurate or appropriate.

All organizations, people, animals, or divine or diabolical beings referenced in this book and on its cover own their legal stuff. The publisher, author, and this book are not legally associated with any organization, animal, or divine or diabolical being mentioned in this book. And unfortunately, none of them referenced within this book have endorsed it. But maybe someday they will ... or maybe not.

*SO, WHO OWNS THIS? I do. Tim Windsor.
I finally published it in the year 2023.
And that's quite amazing because I wasn't sure
I would ever get this thing done.*

HARD COVER ISBN Number: 978-1-989148-10-5

*Published by Transatlantic Publishing,
an Imprint of Historical Branding Solutions Inc.
93 Anvil Street, Kitchener, Ontario, Canada N2P 1X8
(Printed in Canada)*

© Copyright **- TIMOTHY S. WINDSOR 2023**

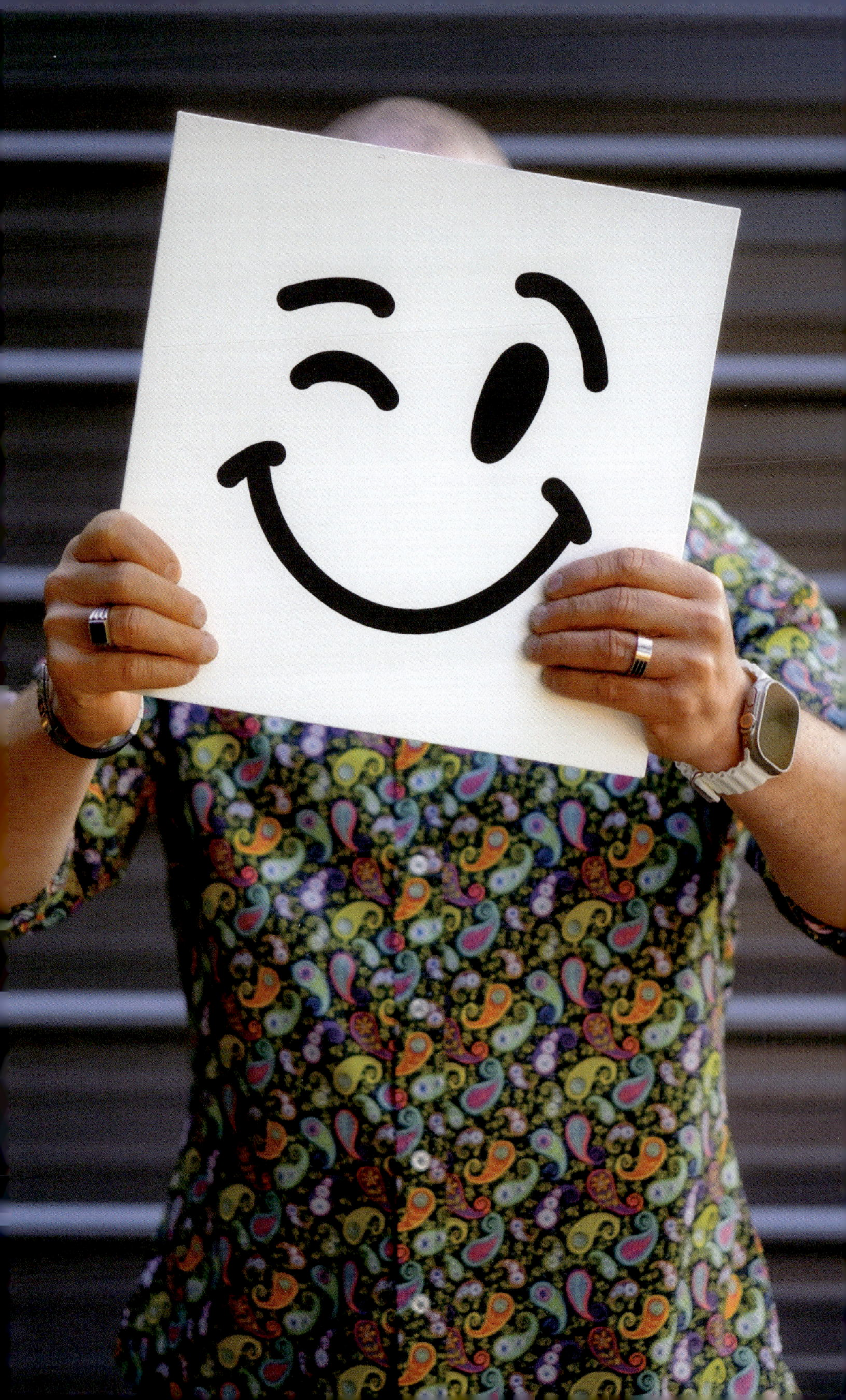

NODS, WINKS, & KUDOS

I want to thank the incredibly unique Homo sapiens who inspired me to write this book and kicked my ass to get it done.

Mike, you lit a fire under my ass in Las Vegas in January 2020 when you explained why I had spent over two years "trying" to write this book and had nothing but an outline. I was struggling to create it with the wrong appendage. You wisely encouraged me to use my tongue, not my fat typing fingers, to get all this out of my head. Thanks for that advice because it set me free and everything in motion.

Livia, you had the most challenging job of all. You took my meandering audio file transcriptions and made sense of my ramblings to make that first draft an excellent foundation and framework to start the journey. Thanks for your careful first edit that didn't erase my voice as my spoken words became text. Your additional edits and suggestions along the way have continued to make this work come to life.

Craig, your regular check-ins to ask, "how's the book coming" were just annoying enough to push me when I wanted to give up. Thanks for your thoughtful reading of the drafts I sent you along the way and your great suggestions to improve its flow and form.

Kris, you rocked the edit of draft version six for me. I was amazed at how many fucking errors and awkward sentences were still in that version. Your editing notes offered me incredible encouragement and provocative suggestions that have made their way to this final version. I hope you do not want some of my royalties because you are not getting any.

Maria, words fall short of expressing my gratitude for all your literary wisdom. I apologize for the extra grey hairs I put on your head as you slashed and chopped my compounds (there's another one for you), tense and pronoun gyrations, and the confusion I caused when you were no longer sure what "this" was supposed to be referring to in the sentence you were reading over and over again. You put your heart and soul into these pages for me, and your thoughtful questions caused me to edit and rewrite many sections with a greater appreciation and passion for my readers.

Aidan, your kick-ass design skills have brought this book to life. You UNCOMMODiFiED the shit out of the boring and bland text file I sent you. I love you, man.

Ulli, I am forever grateful for your publishing wisdom, book design, and printing advice. Thanks for being my publisher and friend.

My UNCOMMODiFiED mentors and gurus who inspire me to live a larger and more expansive life than I ever could have imagined, I will make you proud. I will stand up and stand out in the crowded world and break the evil spell of sameness.

And, of course, **my wild and wonderful family; Pam, Melissa, Andrew, Chris, Emily, Jude, Gwen, Manny the Cat, and Jack the Dog.** You have endured my UNCOMMODiFiED journey for years. This book is a testimony to what someone like me can do when they know they have fans in the stands that cheer them on, even when they are crawling across the finish line, the lights are off, and everyone else has left the stadium. Thanks for carrying me when I cannot walk and being honest with me when no one else is. It's an honour to run the race with all of you.

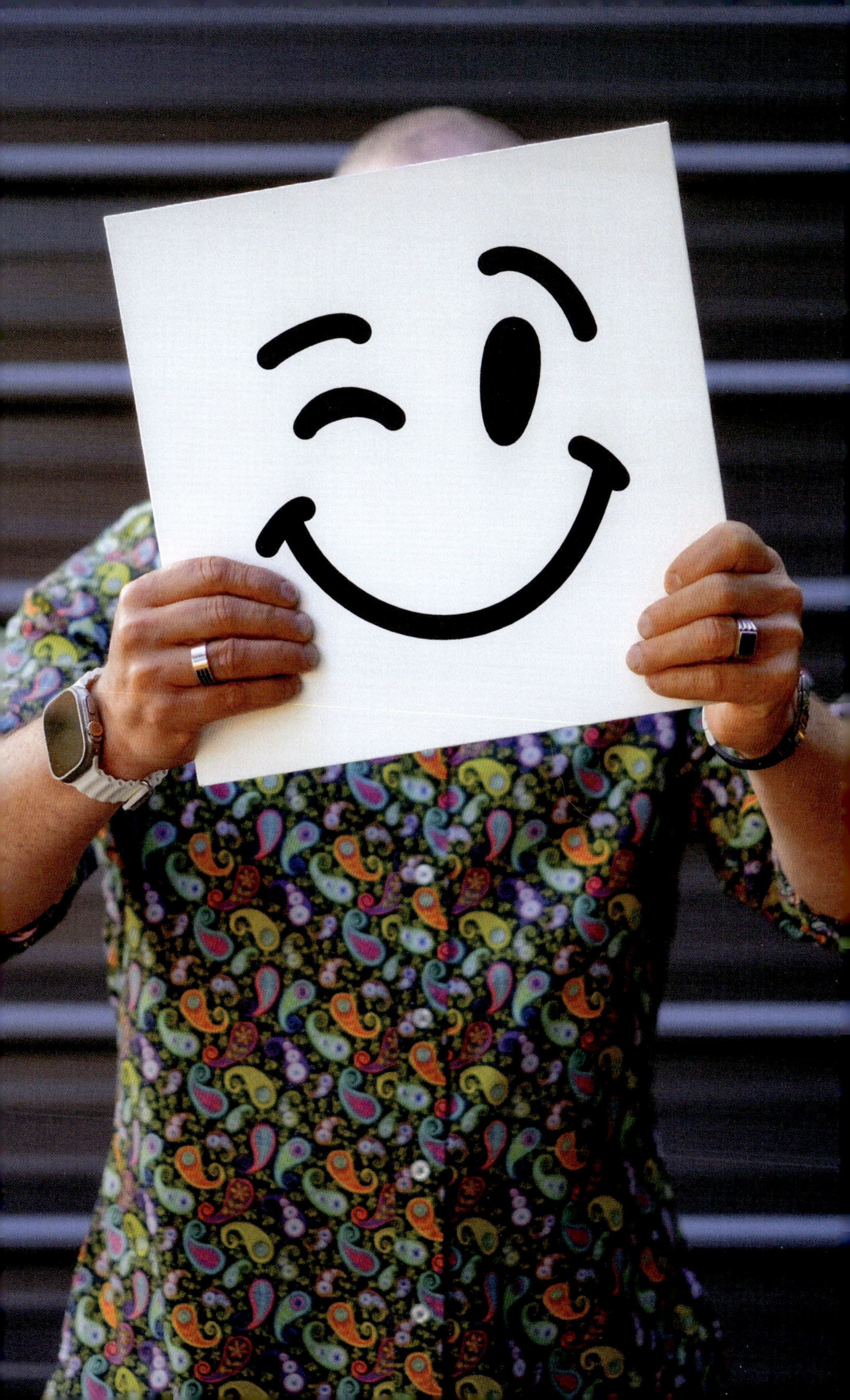

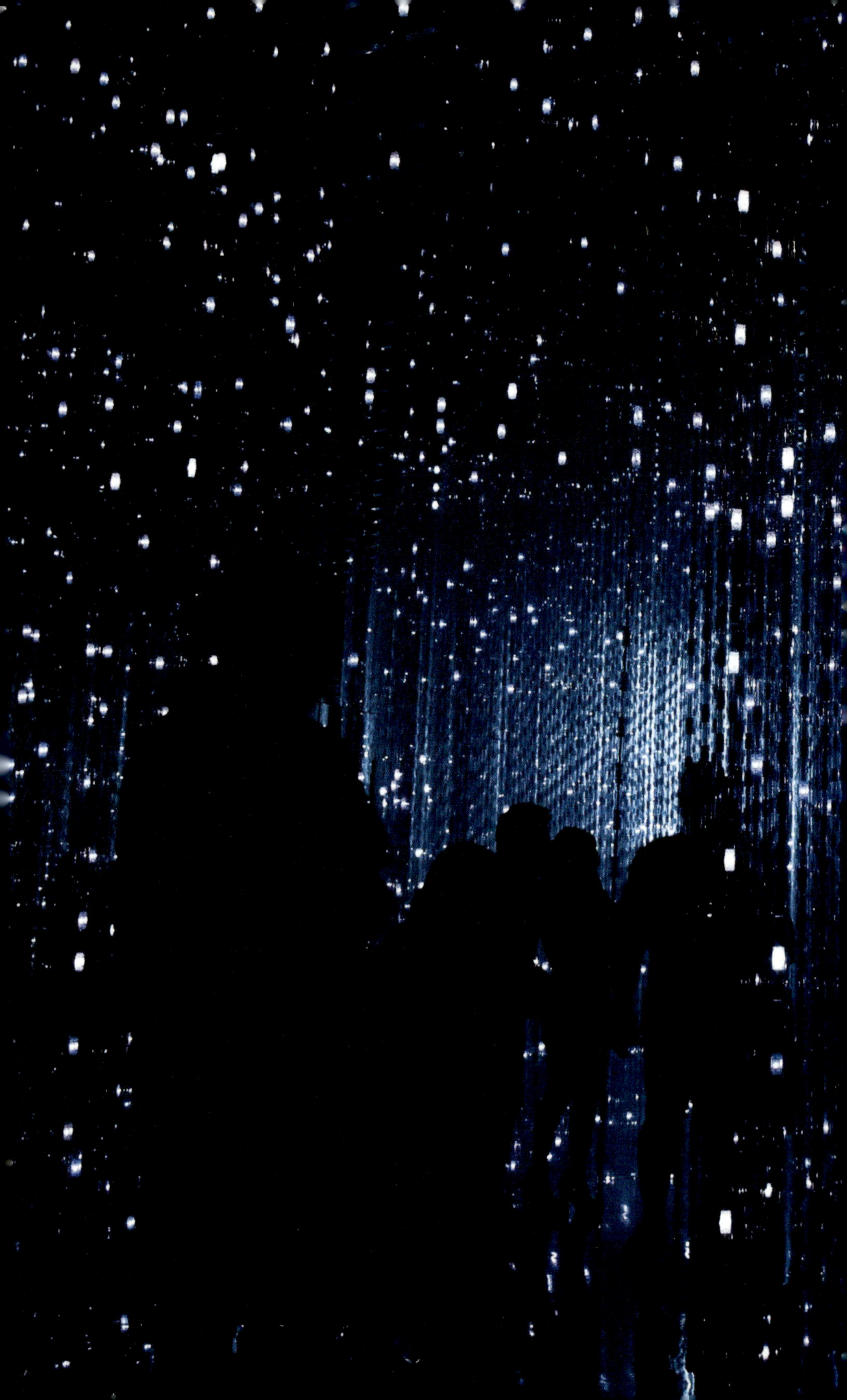

SO, WHAT IS IN THIS BOOK?
(Where to find stuff and some little teasers.)

CHAPTER ONE: PAGE # 14
THE JOURNEY BEGINS ...
(Buckle up ... and get ready for the ride.)

CHAPTER TWO: PAGE # 22
You are a UNIQUE Homo sapien, not just a Homogeneous Human
(Now that's a rather exciting title, but what the hell does it mean?)

CHAPTER THREE: PAGE # 32
UNTRUTHS that will put you into a Commodity Coma
(When you realize you believe some of these UNTRUTHS, you may wake up and not be very happy.)

CHAPTER FOUR: PAGE # 46
The UNCOMMODiFiED are UNFORGETTABLE
(Don't forget to read this chapter, or people may just forget you.)

CHAPTER FIVE: PAGE # 82
The UNCOMMODiFiED are UNCOMMONLY INSPIRING and INFLUENTIAL
(This is a rather long chapter, but I guarantee you will be inspired to read it all.)

CHAPTER SIX: PAGE # 140
The UNCOMMODiFiED are UNDETERRED and UNDENiED
(This is the chapter that will give you the chutzpah to keep on going ... and going.)

CHAPTER SEVEN: PAGE # 162
The Mystery and Magic of the UNYET and the UNMET
(Before you read this chapter, you may want to buy a magic wand and get ready to make some very practical magic.)

THE NEXT CHAPTER: PAGE # 176
Our UNENDING Journey ...

UNCAGE iT QUESTIONS:
(Provocative questions throughout the book to help you activate what you are learning.)

THE JOURNEY BEGINS...

Buckle up ... and get ready for the ride.

1

OUR UNUSUALLY PROVOCATIVE and practical journey starts right now.

Being run of the mill. Being ordinary. Being mundane. Not an option for me. And it must not and should not be an option for you.

For over 30 years, I have worked as a personal, professional, business, and organizational consultant, trainer, and coach. I have partnered with hundreds of organizations and thousands of people. And while many of these people believe they and their organizations are unique, I have challenged them to consider and contemplate another possibility. This possibility, this high probability, is that their goods, services, and even their ideas and ideologies may just be mere "commodities." Not as remarkable or distinct as they think. Not different enough to be considered more valuable or important than what I can find somewhere else. Not surprisingly, their initial instinct is to refuse to believe it and push back.

A commodity, defined simply, is any product, service, idea, or really anything readily available and accessible in multiple places. You can get it somewhere else, from someone else. By that definition, most people and organizations, if not all, transact in commodities. Fine. But here's the kicker: if they allow their goods, services, and even their ideas and ideologies to become unremarkable and indistinguishable from those of their colleagues and competitors — they will devolve and therefore be devalued.

But of much more concern to me is when I see people themselves devolving and therefore becoming devalued. **People become commodities themselves.** I witness people, even the best people within an organization, reduce themselves to "commodities," by letting fear keep them from standing out from the crowd. They sink into the background and choose to conform and become mere shadows of their true selves. Why? How? To be acceptable to their coworkers and even the crowd, to fit in and not make waves, they surrender their uniqueness and the qualities that make them distinct.

NO ONE WANTS TO BELIEVE THEY'RE A "DIME-A-DOZEN" PERSON.

But here's the truth. No one wants to believe they're a "dime-a-dozen" person. No one wants to believe they're ordinary. No one wants to believe they're a commodity. Yet, if you and I are not vigilant, thoughtful, and proactive, we risk becoming unremarkable and undifferentiated from others. We will fail to stand out and instead make commodities of ourselves. We will become easily replaceable and expendable. And, worst of all, we will become utterly impotent and unable to birth the ultimate personal metamorphosis that we desire in our lives.

Being run of the mill. Being ordinary. Being mundane. Not an option for me. And it has NOT been for the "UNCOMMODiFiED" provocateurs I have met over the years. I have had the privilege of meeting, training, and developing leaders and teams on four continents and in every type of structured organization: private and public businesses, charities, and non-profit organizations. Along the way, I have encountered some people who caught my attention in mystical and magical ways. They are inspiringly different, positively provocative, utterly unique, and completely outstanding in their approaches to possibilities and problems, in how they lead and work, and in how they live their life. They stand out. Their example has called and compelled me to embrace my uniqueness and be as inspiring as they are.

As I have studied and interviewed these individuals over the years, **the ones who impress me most all have one thing in common: they are nonconformists.** They do not fit in. They stand apart in the best, most positive ways, in ways that are transformational. These positive nonconformists possess the antidote to the "evil spell of sameness." Others can't help but find them mesmerizing. Like an inaudible dog whistle, they seem to call out the hidden uniqueness of others as they go against the grain.

> I have come to understand that these people embodied an instructional wisdom that I could harness. They could teach me to be demonstrably different. They strengthen my willpower to resist the evil spell of sameness and encourage me to speak and act in positively provocative ways.

So, I began to test out a theory. To my great surprise, it worked! When I chose to break free from the pack — whether my social, spiritual, professional or family pack — people perked up their hearts. When I chose to communicate with a unique twist or react in an unexpected way, I had a more positive impact on others.

This insight into acting differently to impact people in a beneficial way transformed how I worked with my clients. People listened more. They called me more. They asked for me more. Though money was never my main motivator to impact people, my customers even paid me more.

Don't get me wrong; I have not arrived, nor will I ever fully arrive. I have not mastered the art of resisting the evil spell of sameness. But I challenge myself daily to do so.

INSPIRED BY THESE OUTLIERS, I COINED THE TERM "UNCOMMODiFiED" TO DESCRIBE THEM AND THEIR IMPACT ON ME AND OTHERS OVER THE YEARS.

And now, it's time to share my learning by writing a provocative and practical guide to encourage YOU to stand out in your crowded world. This journey is about personal, professional, business, and organizational metamorphosis. You choose how you see it and where you apply it. And as you do, I invite you to explore a different way of looking at yourself and your world and a different way of doing life.

No *Wizard of Oz* trickery or "sleight of hand" will be used to manipulate you on this journey. I want to let you behind the curtain now and show you where I want to take you and how we will get there. The first few chapters you read are designed to wake you up, shake you up, and create some angst. So don't be surprised by these feelings. Chapter two will make you forever aware of a truth that has the power to unleash your full potential and hopefully piss you off enough to want to pay the price to do it. In chapter three, I wake you up so you can break the evil spell of sameness and slay six untruths that put you in a commodity coma. And then you will be ready. You'll be ready to convert your desire and frustration into new actions. You'll be ready for chapters four and five, where you will learn and apply the powerful lessons the UNCOMMODiFiED have taught me over the years. You'll be ready to use your newly discovered awareness and angst to uncommodify yourself, to become unforgettable, and to inspire and influence others the way my mentors do. Chapter six focuses on hope and the rewards that come to you and others when you choose the painful journey to realize and release your uniqueness. Being UNCOMMODiFiED does not always feel like it pays off now, but it always rewards in the end. Chapter seven is about your future, embracing the truth that mystery and magic are no longer found in the story you have already written, but in the one, you have yet to author.

UNCOMMODiFiED is a verb, an adverb, a noun, and an adjective.

Before we go any further, let's get on the same page about how I use the term UNCOMMODiFiED.

For me, UNCOMMODiFiED is both a verb and an adverb. It is the positive and purposefully unique actions of individuals. It's the act of returning to the utterly UNCOMMODiFiED state in which we exited the womb. It is the unusual energy that we exert to uncommodify ourselves in any given situation. It's the unique twist we put on our actions to create extraordinary impact.

UNCOMMODiFiED is also both a noun and an adjective. It's a person that stands up and stands out from the crowd. It's people who are rediscovering and expressing their uniqueness. It describes a person who may sometimes seem like an arrogant asshole. But that is not the case at all. The UNCOMMODiFiED are just unusually aggressive antagonists of the status quo in themselves and others.

UNCOMMODiFiED. It's a book and it's a workbook. It's a chat with a whiskey-drinking, cigar and pipe-smoking kind of guy, a rather uncomfortable chat at times. It's a candid conversation full of provocative ideas and observations. It must be this for me. You and I will move beyond abstract concepts and discover practical, actionable strategies and behaviours to help uncage the best versions of ourselves, the unique individuals we are meant to be.

But before you sign up, let me caution you: this journey may be more like riding a <u>wild rollercoaster</u> than a <u>leisurely Sunday drive</u> in the country. Expect to be at times exhilarated by the ride and at times terrified. I have experienced both powerful emotions along the way. Sometimes even at the same time. But, as I have learned, you must trust that these feelings are all part of the journey back to who you were born to be.

Throughout the book, I purposely provide fewer answers and specific instructions than you might expect at times. This is because I am constantly wrestling with an unfortunate reality. If I give you two easy steps or one application that everyone must make, it will be hard for us not to all look like commodified robots at the end of our time together.

Therefore, I will always strongly encourage you to choose how to respond to what you are reading. You must figure out how to use the provocations of my UNCOMMODiFiED mentors, not just to emulate everything they do, but to release your unique expression of the wisdom you learn from them.

To help you do this, I give you opportunities to do the hard work of activating the ideas we are exploring by pondering provocative questions that will lead you to **"UNCAGE iT"** and translate everything we are considering into catalytic actions. Because when you take a new and unique action, it will enable you to break the evil spell of sameness.

Are you ready? Buckle up. Let's ride this wild rollercoaster up to the top, over the edge, and into our UNCOMMODiFiED destiny.

Tim Windsor

You are a UNIQUE Homo sapien, not just a Homogeneous Human

Now that's a rather exciting title, but what the hell does it mean?

2

YOU WERE BORN to be uniquely you. So, it's natural and good to be different and unusual.

You must not surrender your uniqueness and give into homogeneity, or you will ultimately and utterly infuse your veins with the anesthetizing power of sameness.

You are a unique Homo sapien, not just a homogeneous human. Think about that for a moment! You and I were born unique, unusual and unlike any other individual. From the beginning, we existed wholly and intrinsically in an UNCOMMODiFiED state of being. So, let's agree we are not commodities at our core and in our very essence. We are different from anyone else on the planet. And yet, biologically, we are 99.9% identical.[1] Within that tiny ocean of our unique 0.1%, a vast world of differences, unique possibilities, and opportunities swim.

"There isn't anyone else like you on the planet. You were born intrinsically in an UNCOMMODiFiED state.

Yet, here's the sad truth: most of us have developed amnesia and forgotten who we are and how unique we are."

So, what uniqueness exists in that 0.1% of DNA difference?

Well, my fingerprints, your fingerprints. No two people have the exact patterns, loops, whirls, and arches on their fingertips. Not even identical twins who share the same DNA share fingerprints.

The same is true of retinas and irises. Again, unique. When a fetus opens and closes its developing eyes, the iris tissue tightens and folds, forming individual textural patterns[2], not unlike the uniqueness seen in snowflakes.

My voice, your voice, in its frequency, tonality, and intensity, is unique.

If we put ink on our lips and then pressed them onto a piece of paper, we would be left with an impression like a barcode,[3] exclusive to you and me.

My odour, your odour, whether pleasant or unpleasant, is one-of-a-kind.

My ears and yours. Unique. Did you know that by analyzing how light reflects off your ear rims, you could be identified in a group with 99.6% accuracy?[4] How amazing.

All of this affirms that we were born utterly unique and different from one another. You are at your core and, in your essence, not a commodity — not easily accessible somewhere else because there isn't anyone else like you on the planet. You were born intrinsically in an UNCOMMODiFiED state.

Yet, here's the sad truth: most of us have developed amnesia and forgotten who we are and how unique we are.

I had a bit of an "aha" moment watching the movie, *Interstellar* on a flight home from a business trip. In one scene, the main character, Cooper, played by Matthew McConaughey, leans back in a chair against his house. He takes a slow drink of his beer and painfully admits something to himself: *"We have forgotten who we are — explorers, pioneers, not caretakers. We used to look up at the sky and wonder at our place in the stars, but now, we just look down and worry about our place in the dirt."* – Cooper (Matthew McConaughey, Interstellar).

His words impacted me so profoundly. I paused the movie to jot them down on my iPad. Like Cooper, I passionately believe we must rediscover and remember the real wonder of our "dirt birthright," embrace our destiny and demonstrate our uniqueness. Why? Not to win over a crowd or control people, but to positively influence everyone we encounter.

Before you move on from what you just read, answer this question:

What will you do this week to rediscover your inner explorer, your inner pioneer, and stand out from the crowd of people who have settled and become mere commodity caretakers?

Here's what I am learning about our dirt birthright: we are all born with grand potential and the possibility of living a significantly impactful life. When we remind ourselves of the importance of being different, we can hold onto or possibly rediscover our uniqueness. We can break the power of homogeneity and shed those identity-stripping beliefs that run through our veins like a paralyzing drug that anesthetizes us into a sleepy sameness.

So, how do these rather grand philosophies get birthed into our everyday lives? Let me give you a practical example from the front lines of my ongoing battle with myself, a glimpse into my struggle between maintaining the status quo and breaking free to approach life and business differently.

Several years ago, I challenged a long-standing client to uncommodify the process they used to educate and train their customer's sales teams to sell their products.

We developed some fun and engaging training resources together. For example, we developed "Game Show" product training which conveyed what I call "sticky" ideas: ones which stick and stay in the participants' minds. The game show format enabled the training to be retained better than the information imparted in typical training models like "I-read-my-PowerPoint-slides-and-I-am-amazing" or that all too common "I-read-my-product-manual-droning-on" technique. The Game Show format uncommodifies the training experience making the learning fun, engaging, and unique.

> **FALLING IN LINE, BEING ACCEPTED BY THE HORDE, AND BEING PART OF THE PACK MAKE US FEEL SAFE.**

Here's the impact and effect of the initial pilot project we ran: we had participants rate the game show training experience on a scale of zero to ten, where zero was the equivalent of, "That was the shittiest training I've ever participated in, and please don't ever do that again!" and ten was, "That was the most fun, most engaging training any manufacturer has ever done with us."

Our guinea pig participants gave us an 8.8 out of 10. This fantastic score was a powerful declaration of the real value and impact of challenging ourselves, choosing to uncommodify and stand out in a crowded business world. By offering a fun and engaging way to learn about products and services, we delivered an incredible training experience to their employees, distribution network, and business partners that was anything but boring and mundane.

After this pilot project, I began to challenge myself and ask these provocative questions:

> Why don't we do things differently, and why don't we challenge ourselves to break the stereotypes that contain our thinking and actions?
>
> Why do we seek the security of sameness and conformity? And what is conformity, and why is it so alluring and seductive?

Here's what I've come to understand about conformity.
Simply put, conformity is the tendency to align our attitudes, beliefs, and behaviours with those around us, even when we know it is not serving them or us very well. And while conformity in and of itself is not always bad, I believe it can be detrimental and even dangerous. Here's the challenge for you and me: sometimes, we just conform even when we know shaking off the comfort of sameness will be transformative. We mirror the actions of others, looking for shelter in the crowd of people around us. We join the homogeneous horde when deciding how we should think or behave in any situation. Rather than pursue what could be exceptional and extraordinary, we opt for the expected and easy.

So why are you and I compelled to trade our uniqueness for homogeneity, for sameness, when deep down in our souls we are longing for something refreshingly new and different to be born? I suppose the most straightforward and truthful answer is that fitting in, falling in line, being accepted by the horde, and being part of the pack make us feel safe. But, over time, I have learned that to birth something refreshingly different in myself and others, I must choose to break free from the homogeneous horde and the safety it seems to provide.

> "There's often a hell of a lot of pain when you don't fit in and fall in line."

Like all births, there is pain. There's often a hell of a lot of pain when you don't fit in and fall in line. It costs to stand out. I have seen an UNCOMMODiFiED friend pay with everything he owned to birth something new for himself and others. But don't lose hope; the pain of uncommodifying ourselves brings the sweet, life-giving smell of possibility and promise. It's the possibility that holds the promise of a more positive present moment and the potential of a more fantastic future. It's the kind of hope encapsulated in the smell emanating from the crown of a newborn baby's head, like the smell that wafted from my head, your head, and the heads of my children and grandchildren when they were born.

However, for that newborn smell to be realized, for that birth to come about, something new must first be conceived inside us. Something gets conceived when we start thinking beyond the limitations and judgments of the homogeneous horde, the homogeneous crowd. When we act, something gets birthed. When we act on purpose and with purpose, our UNCOMMODiFiED choices and actions impact the world through our purposely unique, differentiated and UNCOMMODiFiED bad-ass selves. Once we break free from the horde, we will become a refreshing, new smell of impact (present) and effect (future). It will be intoxicatingly sweet and intrinsically life-giving to us and to everyone we encounter.

But, be warned: experience has taught me that we must be on guard for another kind of smell, the pungent odour that comes when we choose safety, security, and conformity. It's the odour of our dying, necrotizing impact and effect. Ultimately, it's the scent of the necrotizing of our unique hearts and souls. And, when we breathe in that stench, it induces a terrifying kind of death sleep that will begin to pacify and paralyze us as we worry about our place in the dirt and our comfortability. When that sleep takes hold, it puts us into a commodity coma that eventually leads to our unfortunate and untimely death — the death of the very thing we came into the world with — the full expression of our uniqueness and the full inheritance of our "dirt" birthright, the right to make and leave our positive and unique mark.

Before moving on, reflect on how you trade the sweet smell of uniqueness and impact for the much less desirable stench of conformity. How does this choice affect you and others?

UNCAGE iT... NOW!

Use these provocative questions to uncage what you have just read with catalytic action. Uncommodify yourself today with actions that will wake you up from your commodity coma and break the evil spell of sameness.

Why do you seek the safety and security of sameness, conformity, and the homogeneous horde?

What keeps you from fully embracing your unique Homo sapien self?

In what ways have you forgotten who you are? Are you looking up into the sky with wonder (like Matthew McConaughey did as Cooper in Interstellar), looking at your place in the stars? Or are you just looking down and worrying about your place in the dirt?

What exceptional, extraordinary and uncommodifying actions will you take this week to break the evil spell of sameness, so you'll stand out from the crowd for all the right reasons?

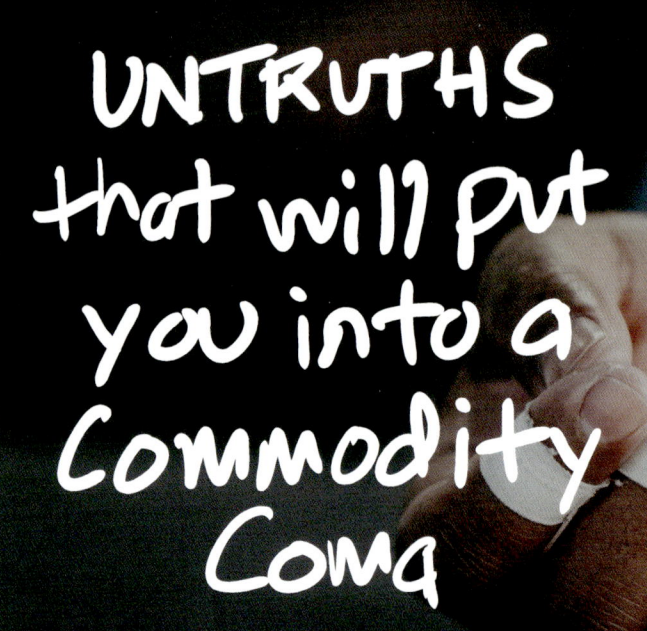

UNTRUTHS that will put you into a Commodity Coma

When you realize you believe some of these UNTRUTHS, you may wake up and not be very happy.

3

THESE SIX UNTRUTHS will put your uniqueness to sleep and induce a commodity coma:

```
I AM NOT READY.
NO ONE IS WATCHING.
JUST KEEPING YOUR HEAD DOWN WILL GET YOU NOTICED.
IT'S TOO DAMN HARD.
IT'S THE THOUGHT THAT COUNTS.
I'M WAY TOO … (you fill in the blank)
```

German scientist Georg Lichtenberg said, "the most dangerous untruths are truths slightly distorted."[5] Mark Twain wrote, "A half-truth is the most cowardly of all lies."[6] Mahatma Gandhi said,

"The more we hear, think, or repeat these lies to ourselves, the more truthful and believable they become."

"Even a little untruth destroys a man, as a drop of poison ruins milk."[7] And Thomas Jefferson once said, "By often repeating an untruth, men come to believe it themselves."[8]

The seduction of the untruths we tell ourselves, which we will expose and explode in this chapter, is that they smell and sound like the truth. The more we hear, think, or repeat these lies to ourselves, the more truthful and believable they become. After a while, the truth and facts no longer matter because we've already bought into the lies. Ask any savvy politician or suave marketer, and they will tell you this is how it works.

You might call it a hiccup in the human psyche, a "regrettable trigger" that equates repetition with validity. Often referred to as the "illusory truth effect"[9] or "hindsight bias," it is the tendency we all have to believe false information after repeated exposure to it.

This phenomenon was formally identified in a 1977 Villanova and Temple University study.[10] Researchers noted that when asked whether something was true or false, people relied heavily on whether the information "felt" familiar. Not surprisingly, the participants rated the familiar concepts more likely to be true because they had already made an emotional and psychological connection to them. Repetition creates familiarity, which in turn trumps rationality. The more we hear an untruth, the more we believe it. This is the power of what we tell ourselves repeatedly. It is difficult to reverse this process once our hearts and minds have bought into these lies. As Mahatma Gandhi said, they become like "poison" to us.

So, let's ingest the truth, the antidote to the poison of six untruths that will kill you and your uniqueness.

UNTRUTH # 1
I AM NOT READY

This is a bold-faced lie. Sure, you might not "feel" ready (who knows what being ready feels like anyway?), but this is a lie. Thankfully, it is a relatively simple one to overcome. We already kicked this lie in the ass in the previous chapter, didn't we? Remember, you are already a unique Homo sapien, not just a homogeneous human. ==You are ready. You were born ready but have been conditioned and coached to fit in, sit down and shut up.== You have convinced yourself you are not ready, and others have reminded you of the same. Your conditioning has made you feel unprepared to stand out and embrace your uniqueness.

The reality is; you were born ready for uniqueness. You were born ready to be different and to demonstrate that difference. You were born utterly and completely unique, unusual, and different from everyone else. As I stated in chapter two, you are not a commodity at your core and in your essence. We are not like anyone else on the planet. We were born wholly in an UNCOMMODiFiED state. Born ready to stand out and be unique.

So, stop lying to yourself! Stop pretending you're not ready. You were created, ready and able. The only question is: are you willing to step up and step into the unique expression of yourself?

UNTRUTH # 2
NO ONE IS WATCHING

Sounds familiar, doesn't it? No one's watching, so who cares if you think or act differently? What is the point of all this "uncommodify yourself" bullshit anyways? Why stand out and be different if no one is going to take notice? Why bother resisting the evil spell of sameness? If you entertain this thought, you are already allowing this insidious lie to rob you of the value you could bring to yourself and others as you stand out and embrace your uniqueness.

When I was a kid, my grandfather told me, "Tim, don't be a fool, and don't be fooled. Someone is always watching." He said this to me back in the mid-1970s, so how much truer is this today in the age of surveillance cameras, social media, and heightened social and moral consciousness?

Someone is ALWAYS watching. People are watching you, people are watching me, and it matters. A future boss could be watching right now on social media. But don't worry; don't lose sleep over it. Embrace it. Let it provoke you to be as positively different and UNCOMMODiFiED as possible for all the right reasons. Be the difference you want to see in the world around you. Be bold. Break the mold. And let a brand-new mold shape you and those around you.

"DON'T BUY INTO THE LIE THAT NO ONE IS WATCHING YOU."

Think about this: even if no one is watching, aren't you watching yourself? So be honest with yourself. Commit yourself fully to your UNCOMMODiFiED calling. Get back to your UNCOMMODiFiED origin. Please do it for yourself, even when you are the only one watching.

This reminds me of an old proverb: If we hear a truth but don't listen to it or act on it, we fool ourselves and nobody else. We become like a person who looks at their face in the mirror, studies their features, and then goes away and immediately forgets what they look like.[11] Now that sounds like amnesia to me — the kind of commodification inducing amnesia we discussed in the last chapter.

So, remember this before you forget the rest: "Don't be a fool, and don't be fooled." And don't buy into the lie that no one is watching you. Believing this lie will put you into a commodity coma and cast the evil spell of sameness on your heart, mind, soul and ultimately onto the potential of your positive impact on others.

UNTRUTH # 3
JUST KEEPING YOUR HEAD DOWN WILL GET YOU NOTICED

Haven't you been told, "Just work hard, keep your nose to the grindstone; your time will come, and they'll notice you." You might have even said it to yourself. And since you've heard it repeated, over and over, you think it must be true. It's that illusory truth effect at work again on you. When you see and hear an idea for the second, third, or thirty-third time, the idea becomes easier for you to process. You read it faster, and your mind processes and understands it more easily. Your brain interprets that ease and familiarity as a signal of validity, and you perceive it as truth.[12] And that's the problem. Once again, the regrettable hiccup in your psyche has you believing a half-truth or even a full-blown lie masquerading as your truth.

Here's the truth, I am an extremely hard worker. I work hard, perhaps harder than most people do. Some might even call me a nose-to-the-grindstone kind of person. It's true, I do believe that working hard is important and a good character trait to have. But it is just half-baked

"Do your work, do your best work, your hardest work, but do it uniquely better."

as an effective strategy to uncommodify yourself, to get noticed and be noteworthy.

Think of hard work as one ingredient in a recipe to make bread. Much like when my wife bakes bread and has to add yeast, you will need to add another ingredient to your hard work in order to get noticed. You will need to add "yeast" to the "flour" you grind at your grindstone. Yeast is an activation agent, and you will need to add an activation agent to all your hard work to be noteworthy. Now when I say yeast, what do I mean? For me, "yeast" is the catalyst of vertical movement. It is the deliberate motion of standing up and standing out, of getting your ass off your chair. You might do it slowly at first because you are a little scared, and that's okay. But next time you work your ass off, try to do something that will make your head stick out above your cubicle. Do something that will get you noticed for all the right reasons beyond your office door. Show people the real you, not just your "work you" — show them the unique, UNCOMMODiFiED you, standing up and standing out.

Don't buy into this other lie either, "If you keep your head down, no one can cut it off." Listen, this is not my first rodeo. They can still cut your head off when you are sitting down and trying to fly below the radar. So here is my advice: do your work, do your best work, your hardest work, but do it uniquely better.

When I train or facilitate, I remind myself to put the "Tim" on it. I put my unique mark on everything I do in business and life. I put the "Tim" on it. In the same way, put YOUR unique mark on the things you do, so people will sit up and take notice.

Now, for those who might think this is selfish or self-centered, I want to remind you of something. It may be true that there is no "I" in the word team — but there is an "I" in the word INFLUENCE and in the word, IMPRESS. The half-truth in all this is that working hard and keeping your nose to the grindstone may occasionally get your work noticed and even rewarded. However, it will NOT make you unforgettable and noteworthy. And that is a reward in and of itself.

So please do not buy into the bold-faced lie that is trying to masquerade as your truth, that just keeping your head down will get you noticed, because it is untrue and unhelpful.

UNTRUTH # 4
IT'S TOO DAMN HARD

Here is what I need to say about this one: at the beginning of our lives, being unique comes naturally and is very easy.

We had Jude and Gwen (our grandson and granddaughter) over the other day. At seven and four years old, I have never seen them break a sweat being their unique selves. It's not hard for them. It's natural. They just do it every day and in every way. They do not have to work hard at being their unique selves, speaking the truth to themselves and others no matter how awkward or uncomfortable it may be in the moment.

Yet, if I am honest with myself and you, there might be some truth in the "it's too damn hard" lie.

After 20,833 sleeps since my exit from the womb (I did the math when I was writing this), it is harder for me to resist the evil spell of sameness than it is for Jude and Gwen. But harder is not the same as TOO DAMN hard. After all, if it were easy, everyone would be doing it and then it would not be special or unique anymore, would it?

Admittedly, being uncomfortable, being different, and being the uncommodifying factor can be challenging at times. But it becomes much harder, and may even feel too damn hard when you allow this untruth to put your uniqueness to sleep.

So here is my advice: Suck it up, Buttercup! As Benjamin Franklin said, "That which hurts also instructs."[13]

"Suck it up, Buttercup!"

UNTRUTH # 5
IT'S THE THOUGHT THAT COUNTS.

I am going to call bullshit on this one, absolute bullshit. My wife would also, and my wife rarely uses that kind of language. Even she would call bullshit on this big ass untruth.

Let me give you an example. Recently I had a great idea, a rather lovely idea. I thought about getting my wife flowers, the tulips she loves. For years, coming home from my coaching and training trips to Africa, I always brought tulips back for my wife. I would pick out the most beautiful, colourful bouquets at the Schiphol Airport in Amsterdam and give them to her when I returned to Canada.

Except there was just one small problem this time. I only "thought" about buying tulips for her, but I never did. So, I smiled and said to my wife while holding nothing in my hands, "It's the thought that counts, isn't it?" She swiftly yet sweetly replied, "Nope, I don't think it is."

The "it's the thought that counts" lie is such a clever and sneaky kind of untruth. It will take your uniqueness captive and put you in a commodity coma in a heartbeat because it will trick you. It will fool you into thinking and feeling like you did something you did not do. Now, of course, most, if not all, actions start as a thought in your mind. Just like the rather caring thought of buying flowers for your wife of almost 37 years. But that is just the beginning. For a thought to be realized, it must grow into an action outside of the mind.

A thought is like a seed that must take root, germinate, and grow. The same is true of any uncommodifying action you will take. Your desire, idea, and intention to be the differentiator and do something unique will also start as a tiny seed: a seed of intention in your mind that will only get brought to life in the material world if you put it into action. If you face this lie head-on and break free from this untruth that masquerades as truth, you will start to uncommodify yourself. You will move from ideation (the idea of it) and articulation (the talking about it) to activation (the doing of it).

> # UNCOMMODiFiED PEOPLE MOVE THROUGH THAT CYCLE AND GET TO REAL ACTION

UNCOMMODiFiED people move through that cycle and get to real action. Once you understand this, you will realize it is not the thought that counts. It is the action that counts. You will discover the witty truth powerfully communicated in the 2007 IBM ad campaign, *"Stop Talking, Start Doing."* [14] (You should Google search that ad campaign – the ads are brilliant.) They're poignant and powerful and drive home this point: Being great at thinking about doing something new or unusual is the starting point. But BEING superior at BECOMING and at DOING something new or unusual, something purposely uncommodifying, is what it is all about.

So, you need to get out of your "head" and get your game on. Do not be deceived, do not deceive yourself. The thought does not count until it adds up and translates into a new action. The pathway is clear: ideate, articulate, and activate.

**UNTRUTH # 6
I'M WAY TOO …**

Insert whatever self-limiting belief or false sense of identity you cling to — your convenient go-to excuse and the untruth you tell yourself, over and over about yourself … go ahead, insert it right there.

I'M WAY TOO … YOUNG or way too OLD, SKINNY or way too FAT, COOL or way too NERDY, RELIGIOUS or way too AGNOSTIC, MACHO or way too FEMININE, SIMPLE or way too SOPHISTICATED, STUPID or way too SMART, POOR or way too RICH, SPIRITUAL or way too SECULAR, QUIET or way too LOUD, PRETTY or way too UGLY, EXTROVERTED or way too INTROVERTED, PUT-TOGETHER or way too FUCKED UP.

But here's the truth. These are all just self-protecting big-ass bold-faced lies. These self-limiting beliefs about your identity and value bind you up and keep you imprisoned. In the words of the immortal Bob Newhart: "Stop it"[15] (google it, it's worth your time). Stop reciting them, stop using them as an excuse, do the damn thing, and the lies will become unbelievable. Stop blaming your past or your present situation or limitation. Stop blaming yourself or somebody else for why you can't muster up the courage to break free from the homogeneous horde, from the crowd, on purpose, with purpose, and for the purpose of making a unique and lasting impression on everyone you encounter.

Don't allow yourself to use your convenient go-to excuse or emotional baggage to smother your uniqueness. **Set it free. Set yourself free!**

UNCAGE iT... NOW!

Push yourself out of the darkness and into the light of your truth. Use these questions to destroy the power of these six untruths, to break the evil spell of sameness and to wake yourself up from your commodity coma.

Which of these six untruths do you struggle with the most?

Why did you choose that lie? How does this lie and your belief in it affect you and others?

How will you break the spell that this untruth has cast on you this week?

What self-limiting belief, false sense of identity, convenient go-to excuse, or emotional baggage are you allowing to smother your uniqueness? Which one is your nemesis, your "Achilles heel?" Why did you choose that one? How does this affect you and others?

The UNCOMMODiFiED are UNFORGETTABLE

Don't forget to read this chapter, or people may just forget you.

4

WHEN YOU BECOME your unique Homo sapien self and stop believing lies, you can refuse to allow your veins to be pumped full of the anesthetizing power of sameness. And once you do, you can never again be easily forgotten. The superpower of the UNCOMMODiFiED is their desire and ability to make a powerfully positive, unforgettable impact on others.

For over 30 years, I have rubbed shoulders with UNCOMMODiFiED mentors that I can never forget. Their provocative attitudes and actions haunt me so much that I had to figure out what made them so inspiringly unforgettable. After years of analyzing my experiences with them, I have codified eleven attributes that my truly unforgettable mentors all exude and exemplify. So, let go of the grab bar, put your hands in the air, and let's continue our roller coaster ride as we explore these powerful attributes together.

NUMBER ONE ...
They are so UNAFRAID it's scary.

Nowhere is this trait more evident to me than in the people I met during my work in Zimbabwe. I recall one man who, when Robert Mugabe's henchmen came to take his home, cut the lawn and asked his wife to cut fresh flowers and place them on the table for their "guests." This so-called visit ended with them taking everything the man and his wife owned. He could have packed up and left, but he didn't. Instead, he stayed in his country and served his rural farmer neighbours to improve their lives and feed their families. His nation will never forget his bravery and impact. Even though he lost all he owned, he stayed the course, unafraid and steadfast.

> **THE UNFORGETTABLE ARE UNAFRAID OF WHO THEY ARE AND ARE NOT. THEY DON'T FEAR THE TRUTH, THEIR TRUTH, OR THE CONSEQUENCES OF THEIR UNAFRAID POSITIVE ACTIONS.**

Here's a question: are people unforgettable by nature or through nurture? You will have to decide that. But as you consider your answer, let me introduce you to a fantastic friend; I call him "Bruce" because that is his real name. Bruce lived gripped by crippling soul-crushing fear for most of his life. Fear of who he is and what people and possibly god or any other extra-terrestrial being might feel about him if they knew. Bruce finally broke the power of that fear, as all fear-breakers do by dousing fear with the refreshingly cool water of compassionate truth. The truth, his truth, is he is gay. And he's also a wonderfully flawed human like I am. He is loved and lovable. He always has been and always will be. And only the power of love mixed with truth can douse any vicious fear that causes us to hide in shame in the corner of the room. What about you? What truth do you need to start believing about yourself and others that will break the evil spell of sameness and shame?

The UNCOMMODiFiED are so afraid of being fake that they muster up the courage to become unafraid of the cost of not living "true" to themselves. This unafraid choice often brings pain and pleasure to them and their loved ones. Everyone pays the price when we are not who we were created to be. My unafraid mentors know full well that staying locked in whatever "closet" they need to "come out of" is soul-crushing, so they unlock the door and step into the "light" of personal acceptance.

It's true; the unforgettable are unafraid of who they are and are not. They don't fear the truth, their truth, or the consequences of their unafraid positive actions. They aren't afraid of failure or success, so they try everything to find the things that work. They step boldly into uncharted territory, knowing their success might ignite change, personally, professionally and for their communities.

UNCOMMODiFiED people are also not afraid of their shadow selves. Carl Jung noted, *"The shadow is a moral problem that challenges the whole ego-personality, for no one can become conscious of the shadow without considerable moral effort. Becoming conscious of it involves recognizing the dark aspects of the personality as present and real. This act is the essential condition for any kind of self-knowledge."*[16] Instead of feeling embarrassed, the UNCOMMODiFiED embrace the shadow parts of who they are. They understand that they are only human. They are not afraid to bring their struggle with their darkness into the light for themselves and others to see. They don't fear what others might think or say about them when they do. Instead, they fight for what they know is right and what brings light to their shadow self and into their world.

One of my favourite musicians as a teenager was Canadian singer-songwriter Bruce Cockburn, who so poetically captures this idea in his 1984 song, *Lovers in a Dangerous Time*:

Nothing worth having comes without some kind of fight
You gotta kick at the darkness till it bleeds daylight.[17]

The people who impress me the most are those who aren't afraid to kick at the darkness around them and within them. And, if need be, they will kick themselves or others in the ass to bring the light the world needs to see in and from us.

So, my challenge to you is, be unafraid of the right things in your life!

UNCAGE iT... NOW!

What are you afraid of, and how is that fear keeping you from expressing your unique ideas and opinions?

Who are you afraid of? How is that fear keeping you from expressing your unique ideas and opinions?

What will you do this week to face these fears and break their power over you?

NUMBER TWO …
They have broken out of their prisons and live UNCAGED and UNFETTERED.

I often feel boxed in and contained in many areas of my life. In contrast, genuinely UNCOMMODiFiED people are so free. Somehow, they manage to break the cages that define and confine them. And they break the cages others or society have built around them.

They stand up and stand out. They will not let their pasts, self-limiting beliefs, nor others' beliefs about them determine their futures. I find this, at times, incredibly challenging for me because I had a complicated upbringing. Being from a "fatherless" family, my brothers' bad reputations, and growing up in a poor neighbourhood were types of "cages" for me. I remember my high school guidance counselor telling me within the first few weeks of high school that having the name "Windsor" meant I wouldn't amount to or accomplish much. I am glad I did not let his words, which were based upon my family history, become a "cage" that would imprison my future.

Not long after finishing high school, I started a small business and then became the publisher of a business magazine. One of the first editorials I penned was entitled "*A Letter to My Guidance Counselor.*" In that editorial, I wrote that it didn't matter what he had said to me back then. I wasn't going to let his "cage" of judgment contain and control me for the rest of my life. I have become exactly what he said I couldn't ever be. I broke free from the "cage" that his words tried to build for me.

The same is true of these UNCOMMODiFiED outliers. They can break free from anything negative that tries to define and confine them, whether the cage of their upbringing, family narrative, social condition, or financial status. They break free from the unhelpful and limiting beliefs and expectations of friends, peers, and people like my guidance counselor. And they will not let themselves be defined by any of their physical impairments or personal limitations.

Of course, not all expectations and beliefs are wrong, only those that try to keep us from expressing our very best selves, our most authentic selves. Ironically, the people we love the most, our family and friends, are the ones who most often try to keep us confined. Maybe they fear how far we might run when we break the bars of our cages and live entirely free.

The people I admire even break free from the cages of their organizations and the successes or failures that define them. Sometimes, the cage of past achievements can become a bondage to the future. We convince ourselves that if our success comes as a result of a particular process or model, that it always will. Sometimes previous failures can keep you from thinking and acting boldly in the present. What failed yesterday may be what drives your success tomorrow.

> Don't read on until you answer this question:
> **What cages imprison you?**

The UNCOMMODiFiED are passionate about breaking the cage of their shitty thoughts and self-doubt. Because after a while, we begin to own the cages others have crafted for us. We start to make them ours, and we begin to fit inside them more easily. Our harmful beliefs about ourselves soon reinforce and propagate the lies and cages others initially formed around us. They are unnatural, unhelpful containers that rob us of our uniqueness and the contributions we could make to our culture, families, businesses, world, and society.

The challenge for many of us is that we are often unaware we are imprisoned. Our cages get comfortable. Even homey. So, we need to see our cages for what they are. We need to rattle them like hungry caged animals. We must become "problem prisoners," not "good-behaviour prisoners." Don't settle down and get comfortable in the cage. It's not a home. It's a prison.

Get pissed off at the cage. Rage at the cage. And annoy the hell out of your prison guards.

UNCAGE iT... NOW!

What cages have you fashioned for yourself?

What cages have others fashioned for you?

What do you need to do to unlock those cages and live in the full freedom of your uniqueness?

NUMBER THREE …
The UNCOMMODiFiED are UNMASKED what-you-see-is-what-you-get kind of people.

The UNCOMMODiFiED will not wear masks or "makeup." When I was a kid, my mom always told me she couldn't leave the house until she put her "face" on. I never understood what she meant at the time, but I now realize that it means making yourself look better for others and covering up your perceived flaws. UNCOMMODiFiED people don't need to put on a façade or a fake face when they encounter others. They are confident and comfortable in their skin and with their imperfections.

Here's what the UNCOMMODiFiED have taught me and what you need to understand. Wearing masks tires you out. Faking it is frustrating and fatiguing. The most exhausting and soul-crushing thing you can do is pretend to be someone or something you're not.

The UNCOMMODiFiED live freely unmasked, like my mentor, who, although he led a business team filled with MBA graduates, never hid the fact that he only had a high school education.

Like the wonderfully unique man whom I encountered in the early 80s who never felt the need to cover up the fact that he only had a grade eight education in a world that demanded that all job seekers show their University Degree even to be considered for an interview. He lived freely "unmasked" from the formal attire that other successful consultants wore. He walked the halls in his trenchcoat, and fedora, with a cigar hanging out of his mouth. He was an "unmasked" mover and shaker and strongly encouraged me to become one too.

Like my friends who have removed the mask of the "right" sexual orientation with which others believe they should painfully continue to cover their faces. Once unmasked, they have flourished and ignited a love for themselves and others that is truly transformational. I am inspired every day by their courage.

> "Recognizing I am wearing a mask is the first step to living without it."

The most unforgettable people I've encountered over the years refuse to wear the mask of acceptability and convention just to fit in. They don't allow their life circumstances to paint their face with the mask of the expected responses. Instead, they continually choose the unmasked path. They don't allow themselves to be defined by the masks of their culture, race, ethnicity, creed, nationality, gender, sexual orientation, birth order, social status, title, position, job description or age. They do this, not to call attention to themselves or make a statement but to draw out the potential of others. Can you hear them calling out to you right now?

You might ask yourself, what harmful masks am I wearing now? That's a great question, and you will have an opportunity to ponder that in a minute for yourself. For me, and I have observed over the years for countless others, it's the mask of masculinity: what real "men" do and what real "men" don't do. Regrettably, I have worn this mask far too often and in far too many places. And this has led me to do and say some things I am not proud of. To not speak up when I should have and to not cry when I needed to.

Here's what I have learned from my unmasked mentors, recognizing I am wearing a mask is the first step to living without it. SO, I am taking my masculinity mask off right now ... I cried when my favourite baker won the *British Baking Show*.

If you want to explore more thoughts about the masks we wear and why we wear them, listen to episode #49 of the UNCOMMODiFiED Podcast, entitled "Maps, Mazes and Masks: Being Authentically Us." In this conversation, Dave Loney (a transformational leadership coach and author) and I dive into the deep and dangerous waters of our authentic selves.

Are you ready? It's time to live without "makeup." It's time to pull your masks off and unveil the real you.

UNCAGE iT... NOW!

What unhelpful or harmful masks are you wearing that keep you from expressing your unique self?

How will you remove those masks and show the unique person you are?

NUMBER FOUR ...
They are so wonderfully UNASHAMED that they'll make you blush.

Some of the most UNCOMMODiFiED people in my life have deep, dark pasts, but it doesn't seem to faze them. They are not ashamed of who they were, are, or are becoming. They don't shrink from the public embarrassment of being different from the crowd. Without fear, they express their uniqueness to the world for the benefit of others. They vigilantly protect their hearts, souls and minds from the shame others might want to inflict on them to try and diminish their dignity and destiny. Why? Because they know shame is a soul-devouring, beastly, hungry emotion. And as it eats your soul, it will also crush your spirit and take your distinctiveness captive.

Here is what I've learned about shame: shame will cause you to hide *in* and hide *out*. It will cover up the bright light of your unique contributions. It will keep you hidden in the darkness of smallness and sameness, where you remain commodified. You will hide out in the cave of conformity and regret and not be seen. Shame will make you give up and give in. You will trade the sweet smell of your uniqueness and impact for the stench of conformity. Shame will make you surrender to the internal and external pressure to sit down, shut up and sink into the background. Shame is an impressively evil force.

As I write these words, I am reminded of an inspirationally powerful woman I encountered in Africa. She had shattered the evil power of the shame she endured as a child growing up on the streets of Los Angeles. The daughter of a drug dealer who people taunted night and day. She broke free and learned to love her uniqueness and live unashamed of where she came from and what she had seen and done. She went on to serve in the army, get an education, and use her newfound hope to bring bread and belief to prisoners in foreign lands.

> **STOP HERE FOR A MINUTE! CHALLENGE YOURSELF WITH THIS QUESTION: HOW WILL YOU KICK AGAINST YOUR DARKNESS AND SHAME THIS WEEK AND MAKE IT BLEED THE DAYLIGHT OF YOUR UNIQUENESS?**

Shame comes in many shapes and sizes. Some of our shame comes from our behaviours and choices, and my unashamed mentors have taught me that you start to shed that shame when you get honest, practice self-care, and forgive yourself. What is done is done. Forgive yourself, let yourself off the hook, seek forgiveness if you need to and make amends with yourself and others.

Unfortunately, a lot of the shame we wear, like a dark and heavy cloak, is placed on us by others. My unashamed mentors have taught me that the shame other people want to smother me with is more about them than it is about me. They encouraged me to use this understanding as the first stage in cutting off its dark power over me. Creating emotional and sometimes physical separation from the "shamer" may be required for a season (or longer). There is a fine line here. In gaining our liberty from the shame, we are well advised to understand that people often "do unto others what they have done unto themselves."[18] So, compassion and grace are always the devices we should use to cut shame off ourselves and others.

Ponder this question right now, who shames you the most? You or others?

My challenge today is for you to be unashamed of where you have been, who you are and who you are becoming.

UNCAGE iT... NOW!

What shame from your past do you need to shed from your life? How will you begin to do that?

What present-day shame do you need to shed from your life? How will you begin to do that?

How will you use compassion and grace to cut shame off yourselves and others?

NUMBER FIVE ...
They are UNCONVENTIONAL magicians who always have an unorthodox trick up their sleeves.

The UNCOMMODiFiED resist convention. They balk at the typical ways of doing or thinking about something. They look beyond their convenience and desire to fit in and live freely, like children unashamed and unafraid of being different. You will never hear them say, "I've never done it that way before!" as an excuse. They live with a wild enthusiasm for doing things differently, not just for the sake of getting noticed but for the benefit of others. They leave a lasting impression on poets, politicians, and priests. Experience tells them that convention does not lead to invention or transformation of themselves or others.

While I live in my comfortable house with all its conveniences, my unforgettable advisors live in tents and bushes. So, it is no wonder they are at "home" anywhere and with anyone! Unconventional people are not limited to the typical way of doing things. They are explorers and pioneers, not merely caretakers and custodians of old, lifeless ideas. They know that pursuing convenience will ultimately kill them and their opportunity to make a real impact. And it will kill you and me and our opportunity to leave a unique mark on the people we encounter in this life.

To call out the best in themselves, the UNCOMMODiFiED crush societal norms that paint everyone with the same brush, mute our flavour and smother our uniqueness. They encourage others to find new ways of acting, planning, working, and doing business. Even in their families, they break free of unhealthy ways of relating and being.

My unconventional mentors urge themselves to be unorthodox in both belief and behaviour. They are compelled to contest the doctrines and philosophies of the "systems" in which they work and live, like the UNCOMMODiFiED sales leader I know who is challenging everyone on his team to reconsider why their customers even need them. His unorthodox belief about what they really sell is driving his team to radically new behaviours in the market. His belief is this: their business is not about marketing commodified products, although that is exactly what they sell; their real business is maximizing their customers' ability to amplify their own proficiency and profitability. This belief has birthed a new way to drive sales volumes: if you purchase any of their commodities, you will get exclusive access to their UNCOMMODiFiED industry-first-to-market online sales "Accelerator" for all your employees. Now that's priceless.

If you want to learn about another unusual and unconventional outlier, you might want to listen to episode #94 of the UNCOMMODiFiED Podcast, entitled *"Exposing Truth & Experiencing Fiction: The News of Nellie Bly."* This UNCORK conversation with my friend and historian Craig Minchin is inspired by the awfulness of 10 days and an adventure of 72 days, 6 hours, 11 minutes and 14 seconds. Craig and I chat about the amazingly inspiring life of one of the foremost female journalists of the 19th century. Nellie Bly (born in 1864) found the truth in what we wish was fiction and the fact in the fiction book that inspired her to circle the globe.

> **What unhelpful conventions are you holding onto that you need to release?**

Now it's your turn. Challenge yourself right now.

Why is being unconventional so provocative and powerful? Because it triggers cognitive dissonance. Cognitive dissonance describes the mental and emotional discomfort that occurs when we try to hold two conflicting beliefs or attitudes. People tend to pursue consistency in their attitudes and perceptions, so this struggle causes feelings of nervousness or irritation that need to be dealt with.[19] My unconventional tutors taught me that challenging yourself and others with alternative and unexpected opinions triggers cognitive dissonance and puts it to work for you. The emotional struggle to harmonize our beliefs helps to create the desire and ability to change you and others.

So, you, too, by defying convention, will trigger the emotional energy required to transform your world. And you will become more memorable as you do.

Go out and crush convention. Do something unconventional to get the attention of others and inspire them today.

UNCAGE iT... NOW!

What unhelpful conventions do you see in others? How might these be at work in you?

How will you become more unconventional today?

> What benefit will come to you and others when you choose to be more unconventional?

NUMBER SIX ...

The UNCOMMODiFiED are comfortable making you and themselves "pants-way-too-tight" UNCOMFORTABLE.

The UNCOMMODiFiED people I rub shoulders with and who are now my mentors and friends intentionally seek discomfort. They allow themselves to be compelled by it. Why? Because they understand and live in the truth that our best moments often occur when we feel incredibly uncomfortable, unhappy, or unfulfilled. Because it is in these moments, driven by our discomfort, we are likely to step out of our ruts and start exploring new paths and more honest answers.

The unforgettable scare themselves on purpose. They do scary things; they live in scary places, literally and figuratively, in places of scary possibility. And they scare the shit out of me!

My UNCOMMODiFiED mentors allow the scary, uncomfortable moments to fuel their courage to face the pain that comes with stepping out from the crowd. They understand inherently that growth and change are often quite painful, like growing pains or when your child's baby teeth fall out to make room for new ones. The UNCOMMODiFiED know full well that growth causes pain in the human psyche. Yet, they remain willing to embrace the discomfort that accompanies their growth with inspiring cheerfulness.

Contemplate this before you move on:

When was the last time you did something so different that it scared you? Something that made you shake in your boots. What was it, and how did it impact you and others?

When I worked in Mozambique, I was significantly impacted by a group of nurses, teachers, and a physician assistant. They brought medical care, education, and social change to their communities. When I first met them, they rode on horseback, lived in tents, killed snakes with machetes and travelled from village to village, bringing healing and hope. They embraced the pain of doing things differently as they sought to transform how healthcare and childcare were delivered in rural villages. They worked to keep children with their families rather than getting placed in orphanages, as was common practice in that place, even for children who were not orphans. They completely UNCOMMODiFiED the delivery of healthcare and education in rural Mozambique. They embraced the discomfort and became the difference makers. But they also understood that being different for the sake of being different was not the end game.

What caught me off guard the most about my mentors was that they were NOT uncomfortable with their frailties. They often publicly admitted when they were wrong. They were willing to risk being wrong to try something that might turn out to be right. To watch someone embrace their failings in front of you is a powerful example. It was incredible.

Now listen, if we could live in that uncomfortable moment, admit we were wrong when we started out thinking we were right, and risk the chance of succeeding, wouldn't it transform us? Wouldn't it change others? Wouldn't it make us more humble and more influential simultaneously?

Go ahead, get scared and do it scared. Shrink your jeans in the dryer and get even more uncomfortable today.

UNCAGE iT... NOW!

What uncomfortable moment do you need to embrace this week?

What will happen to you and others when you do?

What will you do to scare yourself this week? How will that impact you and others?

NUMBER SEVEN ...
They are unforgettable because they are almost annoyingly UNRELENTING.

We often use the words "relentless" and "unrelenting" interchangeably in modern language, but they mean vastly different things. To be relentless is to be oppressively incessant, harsh, or inflexible.[20] But that is not how I see my UNCOMMODiFiED mentors. Instead, they are truly unrelenting, not yielding in strength or determination.[21] They are strong-willed teenagers, adults, and seniors, who know which way to go and what is essential. Nothing or no one can prevent them from pressing in and moving forward.

From them, I learned to be diligent and to muster all my strength: my emotional, spiritual, psychological, mental, and physical strength. And then channel that energy consistently and persistently toward my preferred destiny for my benefit and that of others. They challenge and teach me by their example to work harder, to go farther, and to be the first to arrive and the last to leave every battle I choose to fight.

When I ponder this quality, I hear the voice and feel the heart of my friend, Barry, who is unrelenting in his quest to help me and others find faith again amid our journey to deconstruct and challenge our religious beliefs. I respect him and I'm truly inspired by his unyielding determination to guide me back to a more "orthodox" perspective. And although (at least at the time I am writing this) we do not see eye to eye on all of these spiritual matters, I have a deep respect for every email and phone call from him to express his concern and hope for me. I know he won't give up until one of us dies. He's an unrelenting, UNCOMMODiFiED son of a ... God kind of guy.

Unrelenting people are like a dog with a bone. When we give our little dog Jackson a cow's ear (his version of a bone), he's unrelenting with it, chewing and gnawing on it for hours until it is gone. My UNCOMMODiFiED friends are equally stubborn. Once they have a firm hold on something or someone, they won't let go. They get the job done. They complete the task; they cross the finish line. For them, coming up short isn't an option. And it is no longer an option for me. And it shouldn't be for you. I have learned to go the second, third or fourth mile, carrying my backpack and someone else's, if necessary.

ARE YOU AS UNRELENTING AS YOU NEED TO BE? IF NOT, WHY NOT?

The UNCOMMODiFiED are people of unrelenting action and unrelenting belief. They understand there is power in never giving in or giving up. They know that it is never just one action that gets you the results you want. Consistent and persistent efforts produce the outcome. They also understand that although the specific action we take may not be perfect, it will get us closer and closer to where we want to be. But, to begin, we must take the first step. And the unrelenting, UNCOMMODiFiED people I know will always remind themselves and me that there is a second step. A third step. A fourth step. And possibly a four hundred and forty-fourth step that is required. The unforgettable, the UNCOMMODiFiED, are people of action, not perfect action, but consistent and persistent action.

Here's my challenge to you today, find that bone! Find that cow's ear that has made its way under your couch. Then, start chewing on it again and again. Be so annoyingly unrelenting that no one will ever forget you again.

UNCAGE iT... NOW!

What bone is hiding under your living room couch, and what do you need to do this week to get it out and start chewing on it again?

What would be the positive benefit of that for you, and for others?

NUMBER EIGHT ...
The UNCOMMODiFiED are so UNFROZEN they even warm the cold-hearted world around them.

Now, this wisdom comes from my grandchildren Jude and Gwen's favourite sage: Olaf. He can seem a little cold sometimes, but I find his wisdom can cut through ice and melt away my stoicism. Of course, we are not talking about a 16th-century Norwegian Archbishop named Olaf[22] but rather the witty, wise, and whimsical snowman in the Disney movie, *Frozen*, which for a man my age, I have admittedly watched way too many times.

Here is the wisdom of Olaf, "Some people are worth melting for."[23]

The UNCOMMODiFiED people I have had the privilege of knowing are willing to "melt" for the sake of others. They are eager to unfreeze themselves from icy prisons and melt away the things that numb their positive impact.

So, here's the question: what exactly do they melt away?

Firstly, they melt away their cynicism and inclination to believe people are purely motivated by self-interest. Instead, they choose to believe the best about themselves and others without being naïve. They understand their first natures and others' first natures are not always pure. But they believe a better and more unique part in all of us is aching to break free and be seen. My friends Kris and Liv MacQueen (The MacQueen's) poetically sing about this truth in their 2019 song entitled *"Better Angels:"*[24]

> I'M NOT QUITE WHO I CHOOSE TO BE
> BUT I AM WHO I AM AND
> WHO I AM IS WHAT I NEED YOU TO SEE
> SOMETIMES THE TRUTH IS
> THE MOST UNCOMFORTABLE THING
> BUT I AM WHO I AM AND
> WHAT YOU SEE IS WHAT I NEED TO BELIEVE
>
> MY BETTER ANGELS DON'T ALWAYS WIN
> SOMETIMES THE LIGHT'S NOT THE PLACE I'VE BEEN
> SOME DAYS I HAVE A FIERY SOUL
> SOME DAYS I BELIEVE ALL THE LIES I'VE TOLD
> THIS IS MY DECLARATION OF IMPERFECTION
> I PLEDGE ALLEGIANCE TO MY INTENTION

What powerful words. The UNCOMMODiFiED are not always their better selves, their better angels. But like a caterpillar emerging from a chrysalis, they are strengthening their wings, as it were, breaking free of the homogeneous horde and encouraging me to do the same.

> How will you become a better "angel" to yourself and others today?

The unfrozen also melt away their skepticism, their doubt, and the tendency to distrust. Their generous confidence and trust in the goodwill and good intentions of their fellow Homo sapiens ignite their self-trust and spark self-trust and confidence in others. All of that inspires confidence, unleashing the potential and power for all of us to do better, be better, and do more incredible things.

My UNCOMMODiFiED friends melt away their sarcasm, the powerful word weapon that insults, bites, and inflicts pain in a seemingly funny or witty way. Now, don't get me wrong! The UNCOMMODiFiED are hilarious people who can make you bust a gut laughing. But they don't use humour to gut their friends and colleagues. Instead, they choose to be unusually respectful and refreshingly truthful. They never use sarcasm if they need to confront you with something challenging or hurtful. They don't hide the knife in the "cake" so they can pull it out and cut you with it. No, they would rather cut you a piece of cake and then sit and eat it with you. Then they skillfully, with kindness, use their words like a surgeon's scalpel to wound and heal.

From these beautiful people, I learned the art of speaking the truth with kindness to bring the best and most unique qualities out of myself and others. I have used these valuable strategies and lessons hundreds of times. For example, on one occasion, I needed to confront someone spreading rumours and misinformation about me at a company I was consulting for. I was tempted to make a sarcastic comment to them in a meeting to express my angst and anger. But instead, I invited them to sit down with me over a cup of coffee (no cake), and I pulled them "close" and "cut" them deeply with my respectful directness. It was an uncomfortable conversation that allowed us to clarify the facts, hear one another, and move forward. And yes, I have also been on the other side of the table. One time a good friend of mine graciously yet forcefully reminded me that one too many drinks at a public event is something other people may cover up with an awkward joke, but he, for my sake, wouldn't. Ouch. As Anita Krizzan said, "When it hurts – observe. Life is trying to teach you something."[25]

The UNCOMMODiFiED know how to melt the ice crystals of sameness and homogeneity. And in so doing, they help reveal the incredible diversity of the groups of people they encounter. They seek diversity, encourage it, and help foster it. They bring a fresh warm breeze of non-judgmentalism into every space they grace with their presence.

> **THE UNFROZEN BECOME A BREATH OF FRESH AIR: A WARM BREEZE THAT MELTS THE HEART AND IGNITES THE SOUL.**

They melt the evil forces of delay. They know procrastination can lull our opportunity for positive impact into cryogenic sleep. By unfreezing their fingers and toes, they prepare for action. And by breathing on the cold extremities of others, they also ready them. Their activity melts away the inaction of others, and together they get shit done.

They are thawed, animated and on the move. They don't just stroll or saunter through life. They live vibrantly and fully. Even the oldest people I have met on this journey seem to possess a unique vitality, almost like they've discovered and drank deeply from the fountain of youth.

The unfrozen become a breath of fresh air: a warm breeze that melts the heart and ignites the soul. What a gift they are to me and others. Here's another truth bomb from that witty, wise, and whimsical snowman, Olaf "Only an act of true love will thaw a frozen heart."[26] The "thawed" know how to love well. They know how to have compassion for themselves and for others. They allow the snow cover to melt away, revealing their authentic selves for all to see.

That's what it felt like the first time I met the people in a small Zimbabwean village: people who would compel me to partner with them for years. We became long-lost friends within minutes of entering their huts. Their best food and drink were brought to the table and offered freely. But their playful openness and positive outlooks were more heartwarming than the food and drink we shared. Their "unfrozen" and unearned love towards me, a man who represented the "system" and "race" that dominated and domesticated them for decades, was absolutely undeserved. I came to teach and lead them, but they were teaching and leading me into the personal transformation I would experience by working with them. From them, I experienced an

"THE **UNCOMMODIFIED** SEEM TO SEE RIGHT THROUGH YOU, AND WITH THEIR WORDS OR JUST THEIR EYES, THEY LET YOU KNOW THEY LIKE AND APPRECIATE **THE WONDER** OF WHO YOU ARE."

ice-melting fire of grace and acceptance that melted my heart and simultaneously set it on fire.

The UNCOMMODiFiED express their genuine emotions in a way that shows they are fully present and engaged. They laugh, and they cry. They yell, they whisper. They are never fake. And you are never left wondering if they are the "Tin Man in the *Wizard of Oz*" still looking for a heart. Their souls are on display for all to see, to inspire us. Even spiritually, they live out of a deep, internal intuition. They are fully alive to themselves, others, and even to something or someone much more significant than us. Some are religious, but that's not what I am talking about. They live deeply aware that there is more to life than what meets the eye. They seem to see right through you, and with their words or just their eyes, they let you know they like and appreciate the wonder of who you are.

I have been inspired by this kind of gaze from some fantastic people over the years. My utterly unfrozen wife is one of them. The affirmation I receive from her when I share my next adventure or muse about what could be possible for us is palpable. Like when I first shared my desire to write this book and start my podcast, there was nothing from her but unfrozen emotional support. Her ability to stay present with me when I wonder about the future or try to understand and redeem the past is a purposeful choice she makes. Her superpower is her ability to connect emotionally and spiritually with me and everyone else.

Now, it's your turn. My under 7, going on 17, grandson and my 4, going on 14, granddaughter want you to remember the wisdom of Olaf and get UNFROZEN today.

UNCAGE IT... NOW!

Which icy prison numbs your positive impact and effect on others the most? Is it cynicism, skepticism, sarcasm, sameness, or the evil one of delay?

What do you need to do about that today? And how will that positively benefit you and others when you do?

What will you do this week to thaw yourself emotionally, physically, or spiritually?

How will it benefit you and others if you do it?

NUMBER NINE ...
They are so radically UNSELFISH that they will inspire you to give until it heals.

My UNCOMMODiFiED friends and guides always seek to benefit others. They give themselves: their time, attention, resources, and money. They give until it hurts, making them unforgettably unselfish.

Unselfish, like our friend, Paul, who chose to live outside for many months, as though homeless, in the cold Canadian winter months, to raise attention and spur action for the plight of homelessness in his community. Unforgettably unselfish!

Unselfish, like our friend, Harmon, who in 2010 was selected as one of the top 10 CNN heroes of the year. Harmon and his wife, moved by the realities of rural life in Africa, left the comforts of a cozy life in the US to live in the Kenyan bush for months at a time. In particular, he observed dangerous rivers that made it difficult and sometimes impossible for sick people to reach a medical clinic. Rivers kept children from attending school and hindered farmers from selling their crops. Rivers bring both life and death in the isolated, "walking world." The flood season can cut off entire villages from all outside resources for extended periods, and desperate attempts to cross those rivers often end in tragedy. Harmon heard these stories and was determined to make a difference. And so, he began building footbridges over precarious rivers in Kenya. He is now the founder of Bridging the Gap Africa, an organization committed to helping reconnect cut-off communities. His efforts have transformed the lives of thousands of people. Unforgettably unselfish!

Unselfish, like our friends who enabled us to buy our first home when we didn't have the money to do so. One couple showed up at our door bearing a Christmas card with a $30,000 cheque tucked inside. Another friend sent an email offering a $10,000 gift. What generous expressions of love and support for our family! They are excessive and underserved gifts we won't ever forget.

Paul, Harmon, and our friends' ideals were brought to life and animated by their unselfish actions. This reminds me of a powerful quote from a sermon entitled "I've Been to the Mountaintop" by the Reverend Martin Luther King Junior, given on April 3, 1968, in Memphis, Tennessee, just one day before his assassination. He said, "Let us develop a kind of dangerous unselfishness ... and decide not to be compassionate by proxy."[27]

> "People don't always need us to lend them money, but when we lend others the dignity they deserve, we become wonderfully unforgettable."

People like Paul, Harmon, and our friends could have left it to someone else to deliver the gift or be the gift. They chose instead to personally embrace the pain, not soothe or solve it by proxy. Instead of sending someone else, they set up a tent, wrote the cheque, brought a card, sent an email, took backpacks and shovels and demonstrated unforgettable unselfishness.

Let me introduce you to BC Forbes, the Scottish-born American financial journalist who founded Forbes magazine. Listen here to what he had to say: *"The human being who lives only for himself finally reaps nothing but unhappiness. Selfishness corrodes. Unselfishness ennobles, satisfies."*[28]

Unselfishness ennobles, which means that it lends greater dignity to someone.[29] And unselfishness satisfies. Here's the bottom line: people don't always need us to lend them money, but when we lend others the dignity they deserve, we become wonderfully unforgettable.

So today, go ahead and make yourself and others around you happy by ennobling yourself and them through unselfish action.

UNCAGE iT... NOW!

How will you heed the wise counsel and challenge of Martin Luther King Jr. to develop dangerous unselfishness and decide not to be compassionate by proxy?

What will be the positive benefit for you and others if you do it?

What extraordinary and unselfish action will you take this week to break the spell of sameness?

NUMBER TEN & ELEVEN ...
The UNCOMMODiFiED are unforgettable because they live wildly UNBRIDLED and UNBRANDED.

The genuinely unforgettable people who have impacted my life in the most significant ways are like untamed and rather wild horses. Regardless of what their "spirit animal" is, it lives within them, wild and unowned. They are unbridled and unbranded provocateurs.

Living unbridled for them means they do not let anyone put a "bridle" on their head and a "bit" in their mouth. My daughter Melissa is this kind of woman, and when she was young, I despised this about her, but now I love it, and it inspires me. This untamable part of her personality compels her to speak up in meetings at work when everyone else will not speak their mind. For them, it is impossible because they have allowed authority figures to control their "heads" and "tongues" through the use of fear tactics and the sometimes-forceful tugs on their reins. But not my free and untamed daughter. Her respectful and unbridled observations are voiced, and she is unforgettable especially to the wiser "cowboys" and "cowgirls" on the "ranch." In fact, one senior leader took note of her willingness to speak up about problems that his direct reports had been unwilling to bring to his attention. As a result, he now meets regularly with my unbridled daughter to get her perspective on the business.

For the UNCOMMODiFiED, living unbranded means they are not willing to be "blistered" and "burned" with another human owner's insignia. They possess a provocatively positive self-identity that doesn't just inspire you to want to be like them, it inspires you to become more of your true unbranded self. They choose to remain "unbranded" by the searing heat of disappointing or devastating life events. Their ability to gallop through the fire of life and emerge ultimately unscathed, by willful choice or the hard work of therapy, is inspirational. They are independent thinkers and doers who do not just follow the "brand guidelines" of the system. The irony in all this for me is that their unbranded nature empowers them to choose to be dependent on others in healthy ways without becoming codependent.

The truly unforgettable live unbridled and unbranded like untamed, wild horses, who inspire others to live in the same free-spirited manner.

UNCAGE iT... NoW!

Do you have a "bridle" on your head and a "bit" in your mouth that you need to remove? Who or what life circumstance put it there? How will you take it off?

Have you been "blistered" and "burned" with another human owner's insignia in an unhealthy way? If you have, how will you heal that wound?

Have you been seared by the heat of a disappointing or even devastating life event? If you have, how will you heal that wound?

How will you live more unbridled and unbranded this week?

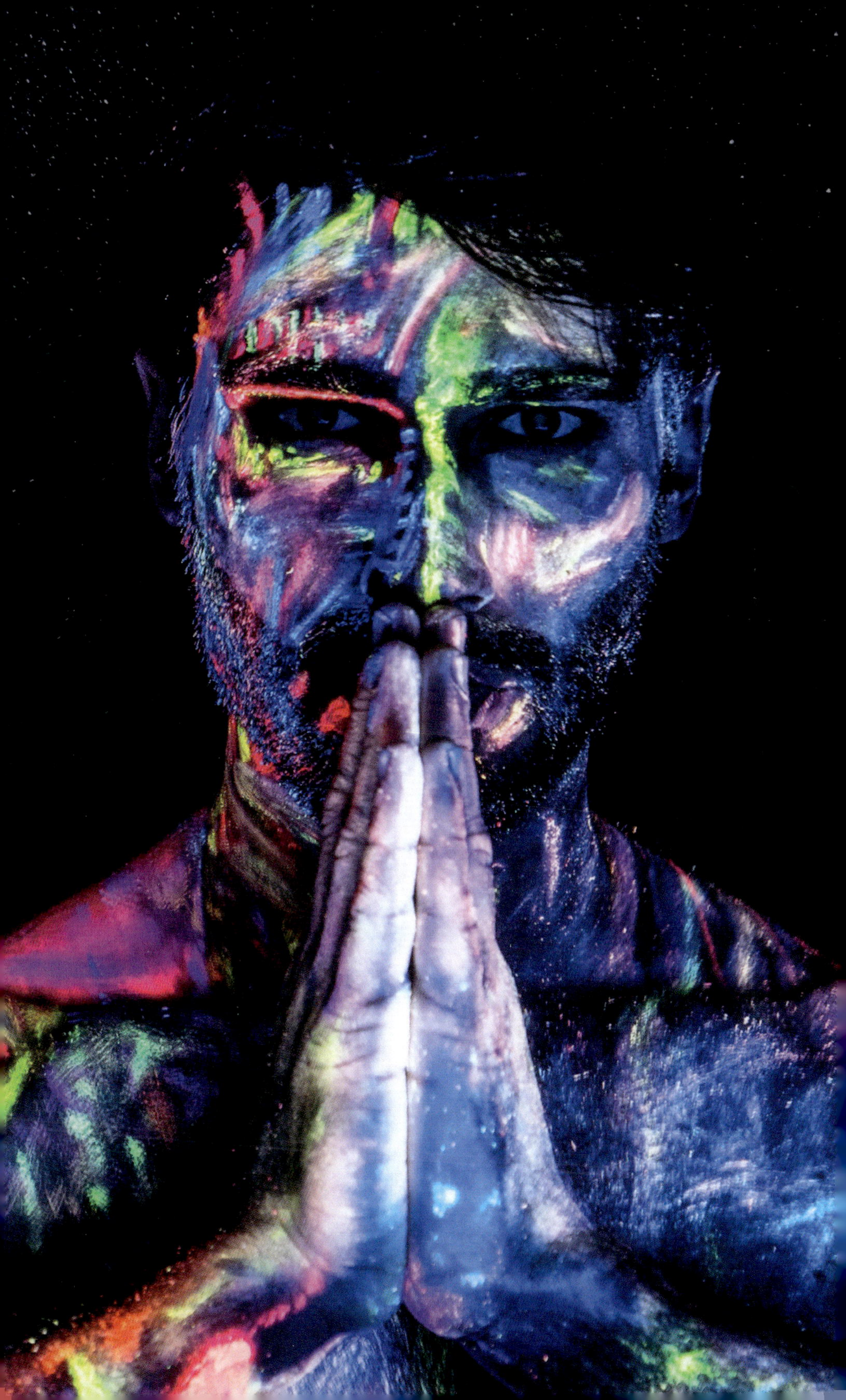

the UNCOMMODiFiED are UNCOMMONLY INSPIRING and INFLUENTIAL

This is a rather long chapter, but I guarantee you will be inspired to read it all.

5

NOW THAT WE have started to "uncage" the eleven attributes that make my mentors so wonderfully unforgettable, let's climb back to the top of the roller-coaster and hang on as we go over the edge once more.

Not only are the UNCOMMODiFiED hard to forget, I also learned that they are uncommonly inspiring and influential. Their impact on me has been absolutely breathtaking and butt-kicking. Countless times over the years, I stood with my mouth hanging wide open in awe of my mentors' capacity to motivate people to be more and do more. I became obsessed with discovering the secrets of their ability to inspire and influence on such a colossal scale: colossal both in volume and virtue. After many conversations with my UNCOMMODiFiED gurus, with a whiskey by my side, a cigar in my mouth, and a pen in my hand, I have now catalogued twelve of their inspirational actions and attitudes. But, be careful, don't just try to emulate them; challenge yourself to find your unique expression of the wisdom you learn from them.

NUMBER ONE ...
First and foremost, they are UNCONDITIONALLY PERSONALLY ACCOUNTABLE people who hold their own feet to the fire.

My UNCOMMODiFiED tutors choose to completely own their decisions, behaviours, attitudes, and actions. Especially when there is a problem, they understand we cannot reach our full potential until we stop blaming others when things do not turn out as envisioned. Great leaders and great people know this. They acknowledge that they are not perfect. They own the outcomes of their actions and apologize when they need to without making excuses. When they fuck up, they own it. They do not hide behind their team when things don't go well. Like my friend who just fessed up when it was him, not any of his team members, who failed to get the building permit for the addition they were already erecting — Stop Work Orders, fines, frustrations — all his fault. No scapegoating from him; instead, he just embraced responsibility, got the permit, paid the fines, and moved forward.

The UNCOMMODiFiED understand that the accountable actions of individuals drive all success. They will always remind you and themselves (over and over again) that ownership and accountability are commitments of the head, heart, and hands to fix a problem without affixing blame. The most inspiring and influential people I have met are people who build upon the foundation of personal accountability.

Great influencers believe in the power of "ONE" and encourage themselves and others to be the ONE. They understand that without accountability, our journey to success will be impeded. Without it, we won't have the courage to put our necks out and risk offering or implementing our solutions. Without it, we won't understand how to break through to new levels of triumph.

Without accountability, we won't be able to earn the crucial trust that enables us to do our best, most UNCOMMODiFiED work. Accountable people absorb shocks and setbacks and keep going. Accountable people persevere through problems and pain and keep pushing onward and upward. Inspiring and influential people are clear about their role in the events of the stories they are writing. They don't fear the truth. They seek, acknowledge, and own the excellent, the good, the bad, and the downright ugly.

So how do we do the same? How do we awaken and activate the desire for personal accountability when our present culture seems to lack it? The answer: we wage war against the propensity to duck accountability by understanding that better questions energize better and more accountable choices. Better questions lead to better conversations, and that helps us and those around us find better options and more accountable actions.

Better questions sound like this:

> What CAN I do; What WILL I do; What MUST I do to be more accountable in this situation?

I imagine all this sounds familiar. I'm sure you believe that everyone should be personally accountable for their actions. Then why is it so hard? Why is it so hard some days to live it? Let's explore this human tendency to avoid accountability by examining an ancient story highlighting the problem and challenge around accountability. Most cultures and traditions have creation stories and narratives. You can look at them in any way you want.

They may be timeless truths, fables, or even allegories. The Judeo-Christian creation story begins with a fascinating account that helps highlight why we humans have such a hard time with personal accountability. The story starts like this: a deity, a god, creates an idyllic place full of plants and animals, wonder and potential, and two human beings — a man and a woman.

According to the story, the god, the woman, and the man get along just fine at first. The humans have full access to a beautiful garden, except for one tree with fruit that they're forbidden to eat. But it doesn't take long before things go wrong. The humans eventually eat the fruit they weren't supposed to, and the deity comes looking for them. In short order, the male pipes in, "Hey, it wasn't my fault. It was the woman. The woman you gave me." In other words, it's not my fault. It's her fault. From this story, we see that when confronted with a problem, we often immediately blame and deflect responsibility. If you track that story back, most people will say that the man blamed the woman. But he says, "It is the woman YOU gave me."[30] So, the blame is boldly put back on the original creator who created the woman. Wow. That's some pretty cocky shade to throw. Through this story, we are reminded that the very fabric of our human nature prefers to shed or push away our accountability and not embrace it. And maybe this is why this topic is so tricky for us.

"IF YOU EXAMINE YOUR LIFE AND GROWING UP YEARS, WHO IS IT THAT CALLED YOU TO BE ACCOUNTABLE?"

I remember what it was like to be caught doing something wrong. My immediate response was to blame and not admit fault. It seems to be part of my basic human instinct. Along the way, my mom showed me what personal accountability was. When I was a teenager, I stole work boots from the garbage container of a shoe factory in the town where I grew up, because I wanted to be "cool". I also stole the top of a flashing construction traffic sign to put in my "party room." "Just garbage boots," I thought — "who would miss them? Just one little sign — who cares?" Well, apparently, my mom did. Both times she "strongly encouraged" me to do the right thing. So, off we went to confess and make amends to the factory General Manager and the City Public Works Department Manager. Here's what I learned from these accountability "encouragements" I received from my mom: if you own up and fess up, it might be a bit embarrassing, but in the end, it just hurts everyone less.

Now, my question is, if you examine your life and growing-up years, who is it that called you to be accountable? Who spoke into your life about personal responsibility? When we have trouble keeping ourselves accountable, we may need someone else to help us. Every day I do my best to be fully accountable for my actions. But some days, I still need help. Sometimes it's my children. Sometimes it's my wife. Sometimes other people call me to account as my mother did. Who helps to keep you accountable? Think about a time that you were or were not held accountable for an action as a child or teenager. Revisit that experience and the lessons you learned.

Shortly before my wife and I married in 1986, she was hit by a car. She was driving to a roadside postal box to drop off a letter. She stopped and, without looking, got out of her car. She was immediately struck by an oncoming vehicle and could have been killed instantly, but she wasn't. It was traumatic, and she needed several surgeries to repair her damaged leg. The man who struck her was devastated and came to see her at the hospital. He was an emotional wreck.

After my wife left the hospital, an insurance agent visited us. He counseled us to sue the driver because of my wife's pain and suffering from the accident. But you know what? I remember sitting down with my wife-to-be and reflecting on this question: How could we sue that man? How could we sue him when it wasn't his fault? It was 100% my wife's fault that she opened the door and walked in front of him, not his fault. He was driving his car. He wasn't even speeding. He was just moving his car down the road, and a woman walked right out in front of him. There was nothing he could have done.

And I remember having a weird sense that my wife could profit by making someone else pay for her mistake. But that just didn't seem right to us. We don't always have to make someone else pay for it, do we? Here is the bottom line: if you want to be accountable, you need to fight against your nature to make someone else pay. Responsibility and accountability are yours and mine to own. So let's own them.

==Personal accountability is expensive== because it costs to fix your mistakes. I remember being at a trade show for one of my customers, helping them experiment with new ideas for their business. I was ill-equipped for the trade show and knew it. I needed to put a piece of equipment together, which I hadn't done before, and it broke while I was assembling it. Now, I could have blamed them for sending me a piece of equipment I'd never seen before and for not training me properly. But the fact is that I chose to attempt to put it together on my own, and I broke it. I could have blamed all these other factors, but it was my fault, and I accepted that. I knew I wasn't prepared. I knew I was inadequately trained. I didn't understand this piece of equipment. I should have just said, "No, I'm not doing this. It's beyond my scope." But of course, I am a man, so I said, "Sure, I can do this!" and broke it. And so after the show, I sent it out to

> **"I CAN CONTROL MY DESTINY BY CHOOSING TO BE RESPONSIBLE FOR MY ACTIONS."**

one of the company's local distributors and asked them to repair it. I gave them my credit card number, letting them know I would pay for it. When the Vice President of Sales for that company found out what I did, he said, "Tim, you didn't need to do that. We would have paid to get it fixed." I remember saying, "Matt, I know you would have, but you didn't break it. I did. I broke it." And he said, "Yeah, but you didn't do it on purpose." I replied, "Of course, I didn't do it on purpose. But I still broke it. It was my accident, and therefore I needed to fix it."

When we embrace our accountability and responsibility, it costs us something. In this case, it cost me $454.87. But here's the great thing: Whenever I have taken accountability, even if it cost me something, the reward of embracing my responsibility has always been more significant than any personal cost incurred. Accountability feels expensive up front, but it pays in the end because when people see you owning up to your actions and attitudes, you receive the greatest reward: trust. People trust you more and believe in you more. They see you as honest and willing to admit you are the source of the problem and that you are taking steps to fix things.

My mentors taught me the wonderful truth that I can control my destiny by choosing to be responsible for my actions. Control can be a great thing. I control my future by choosing to be responsible for my actions. Sometimes it's rewarding. Sometimes there's a cost. But it's always empowering. At the end of the day, I am becoming a better person. I am uncommodifying myself by standing up and out in new ways, even when the going gets tough.

Consider this question before proceeding: Do you inspire personal accountability in others? If yes, how do you do that? What's your process? And if not, how will you do it more effectively?

I'm responsible for my choices, and you for yours. We need to own the decisions we make. That is the nitty-gritty, the simple truth of accountability. It's all about ownership: owning our actions, owning our behaviours, and owning our choices. It's not about lecturing ourselves or pulling out the whip and lashing our backs. It is about asking better questions, which include us in the answer and the outcome.

My UNCOMMODiFiED tutors have taught me a simple model that keeps me accountable for my results and outcomes. It's not rocket science. In fact, it's stupidly simple, but it isn't easy. I practice it every day to encourage myself and my customers toward accountability. Let me share it here with you. It's all about the 3 Rs: Reality, Responsibility, and Response.

Reality
First, ask yourself: have I embraced my reality? Have I embraced the truth of the situation? Accountability is impossible if you lie to yourself or others. We must embrace the truth to be accountable for our decisions and actions. Sometimes, reality paints a bright picture. Great. Sometimes, the reality of the situation might be difficult or painful. Regardless, we need to live in the truth of the problem and its cause, particularly if we catch ourselves wanting to dodge responsibility for it. Lying won't help us move forward. We must orient ourselves toward accountability, like a compass pointing to True North. So, here's my first encouragement to you. Remember that lying to yourself and others will only move you further from your ability to practice personal accountability.

Responsibility

Secondly, after you embrace the truth of the situation and its cause, ask yourself challenging questions that might just (will) put you on the hook: "What's my role in this? And how am I responsible for this?" That's the question. Very simple. So damn hard. It's the question I would encourage you to ask yourself if you want to move toward accountability and embrace reality. Ask the question that dares you to accept responsibility and the truth of your role in the problem or event. Ask yourself the question you hope no one else asks. Because the more you push away your connection to the problem, the more quickly you remove yourself from the solution.

Here's the simple truth about accountability: You cannot take personal accountability for something you choose not to own. If you don't own it (whatever that it is), on some level, you won't choose to be responsible for it. And so understanding and owning are critical to setting yourself up to embrace accountability.

Response

And lastly, it's not enough to accept the reality of the truth and embrace our responsibility. Accountability is not merely a thought. It's not just a feeling. We now need to choose a positive response to help us move forward and do something accountable. It's all too easy to take that honest reality that we've just taken responsibility for, weaponize it and start to beat ourselves up with it. True accountability requires something more of us. It must become a positive action. The final thing we need to do is enact our response.

This is where we come to grips with the truth. "What positive action must I take to move towards a solution, owning the problem, and solving the problem."

By asking better questions: "How will I make this better?" "How will I own this?" and "How will I solve this problem?" you become the answer. That's the litmus test and what will catapult you toward personal accountability.

I use this simple, three-step model daily to uncommodify myself and stand out from the crowd. I challenge you to banish blame: blame of yourself and others. You must put an end to your victim mentality and the idea that nothing is ever your fault. You need to stop hiding from your responsibility and own it, all of it, the good, the bad, the ugly and the amazing. Embrace your personal accountability and responsibility and encourage others to do the same.

UNCAGE iT... NOW!

How personally accountable do you feel when things do not go well? Do you like your answer to this question? If you don't, what are you going to do about that?

How personally accountable do you feel when things go well? Do you like your answer to this question? If you don't, what are you going to do about that?

Which of the R's (Reality, Responsibility or Response) do you have the most difficulty embracing? Why? What will you do differently in that area, and what positive benefit will that have?

The Three Rs:

Reality
Responsibility
Response

**Admit Reality • Embrace Responsibility
Enact our Response**

NUMBER TWO ...
The UNCOMMODiFiED are always UNUSUALLY PERPLEXED; they spend most of their day scratching their head and questioning their last question.

The UNCOMMODiFiED influencers I have had the privilege to encounter operate from a place of great uncertainty as if they are looking for a missing puzzle piece. They are curious by nature, allowing that curiosity to drive them. They heed the counsel of English theoretical physicist Stephen Hawking: "Look up to the stars, not at your feet. Try to make sense of what you see and wonder about what makes the universe exist. Be curious."[31]

The UNCOMMODiFiED are unashamed of their uncertainty because they know it is the pathway to possibility. They are wonderfully comfortable with not having all the answers, even if they are paid and expected to have them. They understand that inviting more people into the process of discovery and exploration of ideas will create better results by releasing collective wisdom. They are comfortable in their own skin and can embrace the limitation of their knowledge. They know what they know, but they readily admit that they don't know everything. They're not afraid to ask a lot of people a lot of questions. But don't be fooled. They're smart. They're wise. Yet they understand that we are all more intelligent and more discerning when we all explore and answer the right questions together.

Richard is precisely this kind of UNCOMMODiFiED thinker. Over the years, I have had the privilege of working with Richard, a business owner and manufacturing plant turn-around wizard. He has dramatically impacted the productivity and profitability of large-scale manufacturing facilities by remaining perplexed and asking probing questions. These questions enabled him to identify inefficiencies and system-wide clutter that impeded people and processes from creating more significant outcomes. He calls this the process of "finding the awkward." If you want to learn more about Richard and his turnaround skills, listen to episode #45 of the UNCOMMODiFiED Podcast, entitled "*Sturdy Success: Positive, Proficient, & Profitable.*" In that UNCORK Conversation, Richard and I dive deeply into what he has learned about taking organizations from inefficiency to efficiency, from losing money to making money and from an unhealthy culture to a healthy culture.

> **CURIOUS PEOPLE ARE CONTINUOUSLY EAGER TO LEARN SOMETHING NEW AND EXPAND WHAT THEY ALREADY KNOW.**

Along with the other unusually perplexed people I have encountered, Richard chooses to remain curious and perplexed enough to patiently hold out for the truth that will set the future free for them and their teams. They look beyond the quick fix and continue to ask the right questions until they find what they're looking for. Curious people are continuously eager to learn something new and expand what they already know. They are in good company with other UNCOMMODiFiED outliers, like German-born theoretical physicist Albert Einstein, who humbly stated: "I have no special talents. I am only passionately curious."[32] Image that! Einstein said he had no special talents other than passionate curiosity. Biographer Walter Isaacson makes a compelling case that Leonardo DaVinci's brilliance wasn't so much about technical mastery but was instead fueled by an insatiable and unrivalled curiosity about everything.[33]

Curiosity is one of the most valuable competencies in life and business. The Unusually Perplexed start with genuine curiosity, and activate their genuine interest in listening and learning from others. They initiate "curious conversations" that ooze investigation, interest, and intrigue, generating enthusiasm for the work that matters. Their ultimate skill lurks within their ability to listen carefully, speak with clarity, and encourage themselves and others to act on the information and ideas unlocked through discovery.

Now it's your turn to become unusually perplexed and passionately curious.

UNCAGE iT... NOW!

Are you willing to be perplexed in front of others and to ask questions? Do you like your answer to this question? If you don't, what are you going to do about that?

Do you remain perplexed enough to learn and to grow for your sake and for the sake of others? Do you like your answer to this question? If you don't, what are you going to do about that?

What will you do to grow your desire to be perplexed and curious?

NUMBER THREE ...
They are so UTTERLY PERSUASIVE; they can even get the naysayers to stop "naying."

The most inspiring and influential people I have collided with possess a unique knack for convincing others to do something new and making them believe they can do it. They know how to win someone over, not by force or argument, but by passionate reasoning, explanation, and demonstration. They practice the art and craft of persuasion and inspirational influence. They're like possibility-Jedis. They can reach minds, touch hearts and inspire hands to move into action. When they use their magical persuasion on you, they ignite a palpably positive reaction deep within your soul. The truly persuasive are not perfect. They see their flaws first and admit they could — and may often — be wrong. And this, perhaps surprisingly, makes them more persuasive.

Consider Artaj, a business and charity organization leader, a physician with an MBA, and one of the most powerfully persuasive people I have ever met. He invited me and countless others to do what we thought was impossible: help him build the largest healthcare clinic group in one of Canada's most medically underserviced regions and start a small, agile charity that made an impressive impact in many nations and for many people. If Artaj could imagine it, so could we. We believed him when he said we could fully realize our dreams. We signed up and partnered with him because of his utterly persuasive passion.

My UNCOMMODiFiED coaches are most influential when creating belief and a greater sense of purpose for themselves and others. They build true confidence with a kind, gentle, unrelenting force. It is easy to be inspired and persuaded by someone who is personally accountable and who remains open, curious, and perplexed. People like this are much more persuasive because they talk less and listen more. You'll know them when you see them because they will continually and skillfully choose to influence with their mouths shut and ears wide open. Once again, they implore and explore the art of the question as a provocative tool to convince and compel.

> "When telling the truth might not be popular or convenient, inspiring and persuasive influencers are refreshingly truthful."

These utterly persuasive people understand that questions are much more persuasive than platitudes. So, they "pitch" you with questions rather than ready-made answers and solutions, and no matter what they pitch or sell, they help you "buy" into new ideas, opportunities, or old wisdom. "To be persuasive," wrote American broadcast journalist Edward R. Murrow, "… you must be believable. To be believable, you must be credible. And to be credible, you must be truthful."[34]

When telling the truth might not be popular or convenient, inspiring and persuasive influencers are refreshingly truthful. The ideas and information they convey are reliable, credible, and worthy of belief. This believability makes people want to partner with them and trust what they are saying, making them incredibly persuasive people who use their power for good and not selfish purposes.

So, get out there and let your believability and credibility make you utterly persuasive today.

UNCAGE iT... NOW!

```
Are you persuasive enough to accomplish your most
strategic goals? Do you like your answer to this
question? If you don't, what are you going to do
about that?

What will you do to grow your ability to persuade
and inspire at a much higher level?
```

NUMBER FOUR ...
The UNCOMMODiFiED are UNSTOPPABLY PROACTIVE action and nonaction superheroes.

The UNCOMMODiFiED make things happen. They are initiators of events and decisions rather than responders after the fact. They enjoy creating, even controlling, but not in a manipulative way. They make sure everyone gets to where we need to go together. They invite us on a journey, marshalling us to action with a proactive battle cry. They don't and won't procrastinate.

Not only do they love the act of getting things going, they also adore the preparation. They love taking the necessary steps to get themselves and others ready to act. They understand that the recipe for success begins with preparing all the ingredients to make it happen. They believe in what the Roman philosopher Seneca said, "Luck is what happens when preparation meets opportunity."[35] They are proactively "lucky." They are initiators of "luck" rather than just recipients of what Lady Luck brings.

Here's the secret I have discovered from my mentors over the years: it isn't just about their ability to plan. From the outside, it appears as if fortune is always on their side, as though they're able to poop out pretty unicorns. Not so. They are "leprechauns" who understand that ==good things happen when opportunity meets a proactive plan.== To borrow from Louis Pasteur, "Chance favours the prepared mind."[36] Inspiring, UNCOMMODiFiED people understand that through proactive testing, trial and error and the hard-knock lessons of life, the magical forces of fortune and chance can be harnessed, saddled, and ridden into the sunset of success when plans are prepared ahead of the journey.

They are proactive planners. They schedule time to plan; they work on their plan and communicate it. They are masters at planning. Yet somehow, they live within the apparent incongruence observed by Winston Churchill: "Plans are of little importance. But planning is essential."[37] Though they plan, they are not constrained by their plans. They are adaptable, responsive and agile. They will throw their original plans out the window if course corrections are required because, of course, they were prepared to.

What about you? Are you a proactive planner or more of a fly-by-the-seat-of-your-pants kind of person? What do you like about your answer? And if you don't like your answer, what will you do about it?

The UNCOMMODiFiED do not just toss shit against a wall to see what sticks. They know that's lazy and won't get them where they and others need to go. Instead, they believe it is better to have a plan and hold it loosely than get lost in the chaos and confusion of not knowing where they are going or what next step to take.

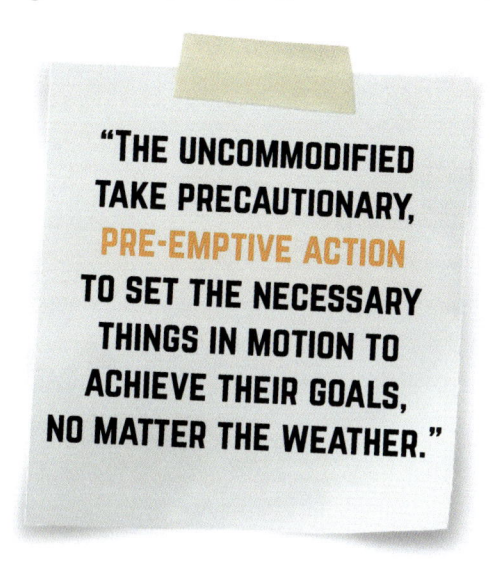

> "THE UNCOMMODIFIED TAKE PRECAUTIONARY, PRE-EMPTIVE ACTION TO SET THE NECESSARY THINGS IN MOTION TO ACHIEVE THEIR GOALS, NO MATTER THE WEATHER."

They love to finish things in order, like dominoes, proactively lined up in a row. First, they get all their shit together. They proactively decide where they want to go and, therefore, create a plan with their dominoes meticulously set up in priority order. With their little finger, they topple the first domino, unleashing their unfolding plan's cascading, predictable power. This is the power of proactively organizing your activities and priorities.

The wind does not sway my inspiring and persuasive mentors. Instead, they take precautionary, pre-emptive action to set the necessary things in motion to achieve their goals, no matter the weather. Good fruit and good fortunes result from all their hard work.

Think of it as winding a kinetic watch (I will show my age with this analogy). When you wind the crown of a watch, wheels and gears are set in motion. The hands on the watch face move because of the proactive and pre-emptive twisting of the dial. This releases a cascade of precisely conceived machinations, and the watch keeps time. Unstoppably proactive people wind themselves up and wind up others to create perpetual motion that moves everything and everyone towards their destination.

> **ARE YOU MORE REACTIVE OR PROACTIVE?**
> **WHY DO YOU BELIEVE THIS TO BE TRUE?**
> ASK SOMEONE ELSE'S OPINION ABOUT THIS AS WELL.

Proactive people are on the move within their sphere of influence, the sphere they genuinely control. When I first rubbed shoulders with some of my mentors, I found it hard to keep up with them. I'd huff and puff, just trying to catch up — even with people twice my age. Over the years, I realized that retirement for these people isn't retirement at all. What some people see as a time to ride off into the sunset, unstoppably proactive people treat as a chance to fit new tires onto their life's "vehicle", so they can get out of the garage and back on the action highway. They are like the "Energizer Bunny"; they just "keep on going and going" and encourage you to do the same.

The UNCOMMODiFiED are also purposely static at times. They are proactive about being inactive; and this is a powerful paradox. At one moment, they are "take action" heroes, scaling every building in sight and then they are "nonaction heroes" who are proactively "unplugging" and "resting" their minds and souls. If it is true that "there is no rest for the 'wicked,'"[38] then my UNCOMMODiFiED gurus are well rested "saints" who are like my son's Tesla at a supercharging station: "plugged in" and recharging for the next part of the journey. My wife is amazing at this — every morning, for the past 44 years, she "plugs" into the quiet refreshment of meditation and prayer: the rest that her mind and soul require to be "refuelled" and ready for another day. On our vacations my wife is proactive about being inactive: a "productive" day for her is measured by the depth of the lines left on her back and legs from her lounge chair. She is my "nonaction superhero," and I want to be like her when I grow up and finally realize the wisdom of rest. Unfortunately, I am not good at this today: the guilt and fear of inactivity sometimes overwhelm me. I guess I need another therapy session and vacation with my wife to "unwind my watch."

At the beginning and end of the day, the UNCOMMODiFiED are proactive about what they choose to do and what they choose not to do. Now it's your turn to do the same and become the superhero you are waiting for: go out and get unusually lucky, unstoppably active, and proactive about being refreshingly inactive today.

UNCAGE iT... NOW!

When you are being reactive, what behaviour do you exhibit? How might that behaviour be negatively affecting you and others?

Are you proactive about the things you need to

be in your life? If not, what will you do about that today?

Do you believe fortune and chance are created, or are they just mystical rewards the universe gives to "lucky people"? What insight does your answer give you about yourself?

Do you have your shit together, and are all your "dominoes" lined up so you can proactively initiate the actions that will create the future you desire? If not, what are you going to do about that today?

Are you proactive about being inactive?

How will you "unplug" and "refuel" more often?

NUMBER FIVE ...
They are terrible at playing hide-and-seek because they are UNDENIABLY PRESENT to everyone in the room.

The UNCOMMODiFiED are relentlessly focused on the present: the "right now," THIS VERY MOMENT. They give the transformational gift of their full attention to "right now," even on their most hectic days. They listen. They look you right in the eye and even deeper. They gaze into your psyche and your soul. They see you. But here is the irony: their fixation on the present moment propels their future success.

I remember one specific experience almost as if it were yesterday. I found myself on the other side of the planet, in a foreign culture, caught in the thick chaos of thwarted plans and frustrated outcomes. My then mentor and soon-to-be friend, Carlos, sat down with me under a large, ancient tree in Mozambique and patiently allowed me to vent my frustrations about the lackluster training results I was seeing with the local leaders who were attending my leadership development program. Then wisely, like that ancient tree, Carlos began to instruct and encourage me in the ways of a culture and a people that I needed to see differently and understand better. His undivided attention at that moment encouraged me to become more present to others and more present to the culture around me.

From that experience with Carlos, I learned that to effectively train Mozambique's political leaders; I needed to be fully present to them. I needed to focus on who they were TODAY. I needed to eat and even dance with them today, so I could work with them TOMORROW.

As the Dalai Lama wisely said, "There are only two days in the year that nothing can be done. One is called yesterday, and the other is called tomorrow. So today is the right day to love, believe, do, and mostly live."[39]

I came to learn two powerful truths from Carlos and others.

Firstly, their "yes" to the present moment, their ability to be present for others and even themselves, is empowered by their profound understanding of time. They see time as a continuum and understand that the past and future exist fundamentally in our minds. The past is remembered, and the future is imagined: their reality is far beyond our control. Only the present moment exists within my grasp. And the more I pay attention to the choices I make in the moment, the more I will impact the microsecond I live in and within.

Possessing sage-like wisdom about time is essential. This is the kind of wisdom my Papa, whose gold pocket watch I am currently staring at as I type these words, practiced and possessed. I keep his watch on the shelf next to my desk to remind me of him and the life lessons he taught me. My Papa taught me to ask provocative questions about time. He challenged me to understand that what I picture in my mind when I consider the seconds, minutes, hours, days, months, and decades we have of this thing we call TIME, matters a lot. What do you see or imagine when you hear the word "time"? Do you see a clock? An analog clock? A digital clock? A calendar? Or maybe you see something more transformative, provocative, and instructive. Perhaps you see time as my Papa did, an hourglass full of sand like the one on his shelf that I played with as a child.

"THERE IS ONLY SO MUCH SAND IN THE HOURGLASS"

He taught me that time must be seen as limited, more like the grains of sand in an hourglass rather than the hands on a clock that rotate and tick away endlessly. "Tick tock, tick tock" without end. In perpetuity. Forever. Reality check: This is not the case with time, at least not the finite amount you and I have each day and in our lives. There is only so much sand in the hourglass.

At the top of the hourglass, fixed in size and volume, is our future measured in sand. The minutes available to us are restricted: 1440 daily, 10,080 weekly, 43,800 monthly, and 525,600 annually. The total amount of time we have in our lifetime? Well, that's the question, isn't it? Whatever that will be, it isn't "forever." Beyond our control, with zero influence from us, time passes. The future steadily shrinks as those finite grains of sand stream steadily through the bottleneck of the present moment, the only moment (the fleeting second) in which you and I live. And once a grain passes through, it slips away and becomes our past, hitting the bottom of the hourglass. And unlike a physical hourglass, you do not get to flip it over and start it again. Your life's hourglass, 1440 minutes each day, is gone. "Done and dusted," as my British friends say: vaporized, never to be lived again. A finite number of grains of sand. A finite amount of the thing we call time. An ever-diminishing precious resource, the sands of time.

Once you start believing that "managing time" is impossible and that you cannot control time, the game will change forever. Deciding how to be most impactful with the time you have available each day will never be the same. We only really live, love, laugh, lead, and learn in and within the present moment, that very thin, very skinny part of the hourglass. And you and I will live, love, laugh, lead, and learn much more effectively and impactfully when we are undeniably present.

Secondly, their sage-like wisdom about "time" compels undeniably present people to also say, "No, absolutely not!" at times, so they can say "yes" to the most impactful thing in the moment.

"Nos" only really matter when they're hard to say. So what do Undeniably Present people say "No" to? I've watched them consistently say "no" to three unhelpful yet tempting options: blame, worry, and procrastination.

BLAME

They don't blame the past or live in it. Instead, they choose to learn from it. Even if they have every right to blame other people or circumstances for why things suck right now, they decide not to. They know there are heroes and villains in every story but choose not to blame either for the outcome of their choices and decisions. With wisdom, they convert past failures into teachable moments in the present. They always learn from the past and choose the better way.

WORRY

Instead of worrying, they make a conscious decision to plan well. They don't fret about the future. All the "fretting" in the world will not fix or change what you need to do today to positively impact the future. Fretting creates anxiety, stress, and strain and keeps you from doing what you need to do today, which could potentially and positively affect the future. The UNCOMMODiFiED know the answer to the rhetorical biblical question, "Who of you, by worrying, can add a single hour to your life?"[40] I learned firsthand that when you curl up into the fetal position of fret, it will keep you from doing what you need to do today to positively affect the future.

PROCRASTINATION

The Undeniably Present say "yes" to the things within their control and sphere of influence. Instead of focusing on what they cannot control and procrastinating, they plan and strategize in the present moment to create the future they envision. They choose to do what they say they should do … RIGHT NOW.

Habitually and intentionally putting off what should or must be done is not only harmful and unhelpful, it is also one of the most value-corroding and value-eroding things you can do. UNCOMMODiFiED people understand this. Anyone with a misplaced sense of pride calling themselves a procrastinator must not know the word's origin. English speakers borrowed the word in the 16th century from the Latin "procrastinus", which evolved from the prefix "pro", meaning "forward," and "crastinus"[41] belonging to tomorrow." Procrastination is the act of putting off till tomorrow what you can achieve today. It is similar to its evil synonyms: lag, loiter, and doddle. The word means to "move or act slowly, to fall behind." Historically, it was understood to mean "purposeful delay, especially through laziness or apathy."[42] So, if you know there is something you should have done two minutes, two hours, or two years ago, get up and do it now! Stop using procrastination as an excuse. Get off your ass and get it done. As my friend from Kentucky would say, "Get on it like a coyote on a chicken."

The Undeniably Present are not fooled by the popular and powerful myth of multitasking, which can make you look and feel busier and more productive than you actually are. You and I do not and cannot multitask. It is a myth that makes it impossible to be undeniably present.[43]

Research in neuroscience tells us the brain doesn't do tasks simultaneously, no matter how much we might like to think or hope it does. The Undeniably Present call "Bullshit" on multitasking. The fact is we just switch tasks very quickly. Each time we switch, there is a stop/start process in the brain. And this start/stop/start process is harsh on us and our brains. Rather than saving time, multitasking costs time, even though that time may be the microseconds it takes to continually switch back and forth in the brain's focus. It's less efficient, we make more mistakes, and it depletes our mental and physical energy.[44]

The UNCOMMODiFiED understand that at any given moment, you and I can only do one thing at a time. Be deliberate in focusing on one task, one thing, or one person because being fully present will make all the difference. Remember, you can't outsmart or outthink brain science.

So, the next time you think you're multitasking, stop and realize you are simply task-switching. Be undeniably present with yourself, others, and the work at hand.

Here's what I have learned: to be more present and to live in the now means not worrying about the future and not wasting my time or others' time. Why? Because time is a precious, daily-diminishing resource. We must squeeze every ounce of possibility out of the present moment, the microsecond in which we live and breathe.

So, be undeniably present right now and play in the sands of the present moment of your hourglass!

UNCAGE iT... NOW!

Do you say "no" to the wicked choice to blame your past? If not, what or who do you blame, and how will you address this negative behaviour?

What have you learned from your past that you must remind yourself about and teach others?

When it comes to the future, do you say "no" to the wicked choice of worrying? If not, what are you worrying and fretting about? And how will you address this negative behaviour?

When it comes to the present moment, do you say "no" to the wicked choice of procrastinating? If not, what are you putting off that you need to do right now?

When it comes to the present moment, do you say "no" to the wicked myth of multitasking? If not, what tasks will you isolate and focus on this week and get done?

NUMBER SIX ...
They are UNGUARDEDLY PASSIONATE; they wear their heart and soul on their sleeve even when wearing a muscle shirt.

The UNCOMMODiFiED are moved and animated by the passionate expression of their unique Homo sapien-self. They are contagiously passionate, feel things deeply, and their passion drives them and others. They are not afraid to show emotion, especially positive, encouraging emotion. They can laugh heartily at themselves. They laugh easily and often with others. They are able and willing to cry tears of joy or sadness. They get frustrated, even extremely angry at problems that stand in their way. They especially get mad at injustice. ==They raise their fists.== ==They raise their voices.== ==They shout.== They believe in themselves; they believe in others. They love people, ideas, and processes. They love the products and solutions they sell. They are passionate about the hard work required to improve their results. They are heartfelt, sincere people. The fire of their passion is contagious. They know why they do what they do, and they help others discover and connect their personal "why" with the collective "why." They've discovered a secret: passion is the catalyst that ignites the actions that success demands. They are fire starters and fire stokers. They start by stoking the fire within themselves, and then, as they burn brightly, their passionate sparks start and stoke the fire of others. Their enthusiasm lights up the rocket fuel stored in their colleagues and customers, fuel that's ready and waiting to be ignited.

The UNCOMMODiFiED replenish their passion and mine too. I cannot count how many times I've stepped off a plane after twenty-one hours of travel to Africa, smelling of fatigue and lacking the fiery zeal my work would soon demand of me. Yet, it would take only moments in the company of my unguardedly passionate gurus, chatting in the back of a jeep about their latest adventure, and my passion would be ignited once again, new set ablaze for the work I was about to do.

WHAT ABOUT YOU?
WHOSE FIRE WILL YOU STOKE TODAY?
HOW WILL YOU LIGHT THEM ON FIRE? AND WHAT WILL BE THE POSITIVE OUTCOME WHEN YOU DO?

Fire starters understand that words matter and have potent meanings. So let's follow their example and take a deeper dive into some language. The etymology (origin) of the word "passion" comes from Latin and means "suffering, enduring."[45] I find this interesting because it is not how we think of passion today. We might think of it as intense, undivided interest in something or an unstoppable driving force, but the root of the word actually points to a terrible pain, a fire that demands to be quenched. This is what the word meant originally.

Modern-day synonyms include affection, anger, devotion, fervour, fury, intensity, rage, resentment, spirit, temper, and zeal.[46] At first glance, some of these words might seem negative, but they are not. Instead, they are full of energy and things you might love or hate. They motivate you.

Modern antonyms include apathy, dullness, indifference, and even lethargy. No thanks. I would not want people to use them (or even consider them) to describe me or their encounters with me. How about you? Would you want them to represent you in that way?

For me, the word passion is closely tied to enthusiasm. The word "enthusiasm" is a sixteenth-century Middle French word derived from Latin and Greek, meaning "divine inspiration, frenzy. To be inspired or possessed by a god, to be ecstatic." Later meanings included "fervour" and "zeal."[47] It's a powerful word. It's provocative. At its core and essence, it is a spiritual thing, not just a physical one. It isn't just about being energetic with words or body language, waving your arms or talking with your hands. It is a "spiritual" thing. It touches not only our minds and emotions but also our hearts, souls, and spirits when we get passionate. It makes things come alive. It transcends the physical stuff going on around us. Our zeal convinces people that we believe what we are saying is valid and vital.

Let me illustrate with a story about the power of enthusiasm. Years ago, I attended a seminar by Uniroyal-Goodrich Tire's Senior Vice President of Marketing. He told an interesting story. His company had recently awarded ten million dollars to a Canadian advertising agency to represent them in the market. They narrowed it down to four companies that pitched their proposals to their team. The executives evaluated the presentations and ideas of each prospective agency using scorecards. Ultimately, the company awarded the ten-million-dollar contract won by a single point. Their edge over the other contenders was in "enthusiasm of presentation." Yes, you read that right. **They won because they were more enthusiastic about what they were communicating**. The Senior VP concluded, "Next time someone tells you that enthusiasm doesn't count; I say ten million dollars."

Enthusiasm, then, isn't just for yourself. It's for others. When you communicate enthusiastically, you convince others (and yourself) that you believe it. You are "divinely" inspired, as though possessed by a god. Passion helps people buy in, get on board, understand, and build belief, which is why it is so powerful. Steve Jobs said, "You have to be burning with an idea, or a problem, or a wrong that you want to right. If you're not passionate enough from the start, you'll never stick it out."[48]

Passion is raw energy. And you experience its power by concentrating on what excites you because if it excites, it can ignite. It is energy and fuel that helps things move forward and upward.

> **"WHAT DO YOU LOVE OR HATE SO MUCH THAT IT HURTS? AND HOW DO I USE THAT LOVE OR HATE TO DRIVE ME AND OTHERS FORWARD?"**

If you want to discover your personal and professional passions, it comes down to understanding and narrowing down what exactly you love. If you love something, you will be more passionate about it. The same goes if you hate something. Your passion will show through. What you love on one extreme and hate on another will drive a sense of urgency toward it, like a pain that needs to be soothed. Begin by asking yourself, "What do I love? What do I hate?" What do you love or hate so much that it hurts? And how do I use that love or hate to drive me and others forward? It's about understanding what you must and will do and for what you'd be willing to die. Remember Olaf? He concluded there were "some people worth melting for." Follow your passion trail. What things can you not live without? What things would you die for? What do you stand for? What won't you compromise on? What would you sacrifice? What would you allow the pain of passion to cost you?

It boils down to a simple concept. It's about "getting to," not "having to." **Your passions are things you GET to do, not things you HAVE to do.** You are neither driven by love nor hate when you feel obligated to do something. It's not something you'd die over. If it is expected of you, or you do it just for someone else, or as just part of your job, you won't experience that same passion. Learn to catalyze your energy and passion for things by turning have-tos into get-tos. This shift in perspective will transform what you choose to do into a privilege instead of an obligation. Here's the nitty-gritty on all this: your passion doesn't always pay but always rewards.

So, go ahead and activate and articulate your passions. Love everything and everyone more, and don't be afraid to show it. Let your guard down. Be enthusiastic. Get caught up in the spirit of "divine" passion and become more inspiring and influential. Become unguardedly passionate and uncommonly inspiring and influential. Do it now!

UNCAGE iT... NOW!

What new fire do you need to start in your life this week? And what will be the positive outcome when you do?

What old fire do you need to stoke this week in your life? And what will be the positive outcome when you do?

NUMBER SEVEN…
The UNCOMMODiFiED are UNRESERVEDLY POSITIVE people that even make "negative Nellies" see the bright side of life.

The UNCOMMODiFiED encourage themselves and others to see the bright side and to be unreservedly positive. But they are not pollyannaish about it. You might not have heard this word before, "pollyannaish." It comes from a 1913 children's book by Eleanor H. Porter, entitled *Pollyanna*.[52] In it, her young protagonist of the same name tries to find something positive in every situation. It's a trick she comes to refer to as the "glad game."

But inspirational people don't just play the "glad game." They don't try to trick themselves or others into a pollyannaish positivity trance. They admit when there are problems and aren't afraid to call them problems instead of using less provocative words like "issues," or even more euphemistic (sugar-coated) words like "opportunities" to describe their problems. They approach problems with a positive disposition. Their provocative, proactive, and positive posture toward the problems they face is a powerful example and encouragement. And I believe this secret weapon empowers them and those inspired by them to blow problems out of the water so they can sail onward.

> **HOW DOES IT WORK IN YOUR LIFE? DO YOU TEND TO LOOK ON THE BRIGHT SIDE OR THE DARK SIDE? HOW DOES YOUR ANSWER HELP OR HINDER YOU AND OTHERS?**

UNCOMMODiFiED people don't wear rose-coloured glasses. They are hopeful realists. They observe the world through a bifocal prescription of optimism and realism. And this clarity enables them to make a three-chemical bomb of positivity, optimism, and authenticity which explodes with an earth-shatteringly positive impact on people and problems.

They love the positive power and possibility encapsulated in the "maybe" moments they and others can create. The unreservedly positive define the word "may" as "possibility" and as "permission"[49] to do what is required to have positive impact. They define "be" as a "state of being,"[50] the way things can or will be. They are all about helping others find the "maybe": the possibilities of a brighter, more positive future. And they know that to create the positive "maybe," we must overcome the fear of our own insignificance. As the authors of the book "Getting to Maybe: How the world is changed" note, "Many of us have a deep desire to make the world a better place, but often our good intentions are undermined by the fear that we are so insignificant nothing we can do will actually make a difference."[51]

The UNCOMMODiFiED turn their propensity for positivity into a powerful force that propels their teams and partners forward to execute the plans they create together. But it does not mean they don't occasionally get discouraged or depressed. I have encountered unreservedly positive people who have suffered bouts of one or both. But in times of difficulty, darkness, discouragement, or even depression, they continue to challenge and encourage themselves and others to look up and see the sunshine breaking through. When I think about this wonderful propensity, I am reminded of my UNCOMMODiFiED friend Charles. He grew up in abject poverty in Mozambique, lost his mother and father to a brutal civil war, and lived on the streets as an orphan. Though dark clouds surrounded him most of his life, he chose to look to the bright side and harness the energy of his positive actions and attitudes to move himself and everyone he befriended (like me) to a more brilliant place of hope.

Here's a magnificent paradox I discovered: The most positive people I have met are some of the poorest on the planet. They are the unreservedly positive people I met in South Africa, Mozambique, Zimbabwe, Kenya, India, Guatemala, and the Caribbean. They exuded an inward joy and positivity that left me baffled. How is this possible? How can this be? Here is what I believe. A more purposefully positive outlook will shine brightest in the darkest places: places of despair.

So, put on some new glasses, make the "bomb," and be unreservedly positive today.

UNCAGE iT...NOW!

How will you change any negative reactions or emotions you are experiencing today into positive, productive ones?

How are the feelings and forces of optimism, realism, and positivity at work in your life? And how does your answer help or hinder you and others?

Complete this sentence: The most positive people who have impacted my life are people who ….

What does your answer teach you that you need to teach others?

NUMBER EIGHT ...

They are UNABASHEDLY PLAYFUL people who will never let "Jack" be a dull boy.

It's the things we play with and the people who help us play that make a great difference in our lives." - Fred Rogers[53]

The UNCOMMODiFiED have rediscovered their unique "dirt birthright." They get down and dirty; they get their hands dirty and work and play in the dirt like curious children. They are work hard and play even harder kind of people. They know that all work and no play does make "Jack" and them "dull" boys and girls.[54] But how? How, as adults, does a lack of playfulness "dull" us? Firstly, **an inability to play makes us rather boring to others, and this, over time, makes it almost impossible to stand out from the crowd and return to the uniqueness we possessed as a child.** Additionally, our inability to play dulls the "edge" of our unique personality that we need to "carve" a lasting impression on others.

My very UNCOMMODiFiED friends Gary, Terry, and Heidi immediately come to mind when I think about some of the most unabashedly playful people I have met. Their playfulness is one of their superpowers. Initiating unexpected water fights; applying masking tape pinstripes to your car overnight; sneaking an unwanted piece of distasteful goat onto your plate at a public dinner event in Africa; hiding a fake snake in your sleeping bag; nick-naming us the 1975 TV police partners "Starsky & Hutch" after crazy middle-of-the-night car races; and welcoming me, on my first visit to their house with a sign on the door that said, "If you're not Tim Windsor – FUCK OFF": unabashed playfulness that still inspires me today to stop "adulting" and start staring at the world with childlike wonder. Gary, Terry, and Heidi are like children when they play with you, yet they are not immature in any way. As Friedrich Nietzsche said, "Man's maturity: to have regained the seriousness that he had as a child at play."[55]

Some people (embarrassingly, me most days) believe that play should be the obsession only of children. But the truth is play is just as vital for adults as it is for kids. My grandchildren's playmate Nanna Pam (my wife) and subject matter experts I have read all understand that there are powerful reasons why you and I need to learn to be more unabashedly playful.

Play has some fantastic benefits. It helps us improve relationships and social connections. When we play with others, we engage in a collective experience that strengthens relationships, creates bonds, breaks down barriers and encourages communication.[56]

Apparently, being more unabashedly playful is like a workout at the gym. It improves physical and mental health. Physical play improves cardiovascular health, strength, and endurance. As adults, we often have hectic and demanding lives, and it can be challenging to find ways to unwind. Engaging in play, whether it's a board game or even colouring in a colouring book, provides a much needed break from the stressors of everyday life.[57]

Inspired by my wife's amazing ability to play and her recent journey into the world of painting, I began researching the neuroscience of play on the brain and its functions. Research shows that play stimulates the release of endorphins: neurotransmitters that promote pleasure and happiness. This leads to a decrease in stress hormones such as cortisol, which is why play improves mental health.[58]

Adults engaging in play stimulate different brain regions than those used when we work. This leads to improved cognitive flexibility and increases creativity.[59] Carl Jung noted, "The creation of something new is not accomplished by the intellect but by the play instinct acting from inner necessity. The creative mind plays with the objects it loves."[60] Play sparks creativity, inspires new ideas, and helps us rediscover our curiosity. Being unabashedly playful makes our brains "young" again.[61]

Play also stimulates the release of dopamine: a neurotransmitter associated with reward and pleasure. This leads to increased motivation and engagement. Additionally, play stimulates the growth of new neural connections and promotes neuroplasticity,[62] which is the brain's ability to adapt and change in response to new experiences. This increased neuroplasticity is especially important to older adults experiencing age-related cognitive decline.[63] I guess George Bernard Shaw was on to something when he said, "We don't stop playing because we grow old; we grow old because we stop playing."[64]

Here's what my UNCOMMODiFiED playground partners challenged me to do: get in a water fight, find a new nick name, turn off my phone, log off my computer, buy a trailer, get off the grid, and play like a kid again. I am proud to report that I am taking their advice; I play with my childhood collection of Lego when my grandchildren are not at my house, and this year my wife and I will spend 15 weeks sitting outside our trailer by the campfire, playing ring toss, card games, and swinging in the hammock.

I challenge you to become more unabashedly playful today. Get the neuroscience of play working hard for you and understand that, as G. K. Chesterton said, "It might reasonably be maintained that the true object of all human life is play."[65]

UNCAGE iT... NOW!

```
What games did you love as a child? Why?

Are you a work hard, play even harder kind of
person?

If you are already great at playing, who do you
need to encourage to stop "adulting" and to play
more?

If you're not great at playing, how can you
rediscover the wonder of child's play?
```

NUMBER NINE ...
The UNCOMMODiFiED are so UNEQUIVOCALLY PRACTICAL even Archimedes asks them to move the world for him.

My UNCOMMODiFiED advisors are down-to-earth people, not pie-in-the-sky people. They are everyday, ordinary people who are primarily focused on practical action rather than abstract theories. Albert Einstein wisely said, "In theory, theory and practice are the same. In practice, they are not."[66] Practical people know and understand theory doesn't move mountains or even little molehills. But theory, functional, articulated theory, animated with action, can and does move both heaven and earth.

> **4 TRUTHS ABOUT**
>
> 1. They are both practical and theoretical
> 2. They are practicing performers and players

Oliver Wendell Holmes, Sr. said, "Some people are so heavenly-minded that they're no earthly good."[67] But, of course, he wasn't talking about those unequivocally practical, down-to-earth people who get down and dirty instead of just thinking about doing something: people like our friends Christine and George who do not let their love of "heaven" keep them from entering the "hell" of homelessness and addiction that surrounds them. They don't just think and talk about helping; weekly they mobilize an "army" of volunteers who provide hot food and warm showers as a practical expression of a "divine" kind of love and acceptance.

Great influencers don't just leave things on paper or, worse, rattling around in their head. Instead, they leave everything on the field, practicing what they preach. They are not just speculators and spectators but practitioners and players in the game of life. As Collins dictionary defines "practical" they are: "Concerned with the actual doing of something, rather than just with theories, ideas, plans, or methods, likely to succeed or to be effective in real circumstances, the real world."[68]

UNCOMMODiFiED outliers move beyond hypotheses and test their theories in the theatre of life. This leads me to their second attribute: they are practicing performers and players, though not perfect prognosticators. Practice does not make perfect, that is for sure. But it does make you and your performance a hell of a lot better. It might not help you tell the future, but it does help

THE UNCOMMODiFiED

They are generators, not just Generals

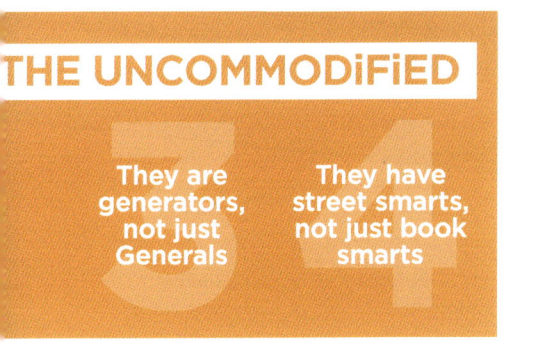

They have street smarts, not just book smarts

you prepare to experience it, which is exactly what the original Greek word for practical, "practicus" means: "Theirs to perform or experience." [69]

The unequivocally practical are performers, experimenters, actors, and alchemists who know what ingredients to mix with their ideas to create practical magic and practical action. They understand what Shakespeare penned in *As You Like It* when he wrote: "All the world's a stage, and all the men and women merely players; They have their exits and their entrances, And one man in his time plays many parts."[70]

Inspiring people are actors on the stage of life, not just in the theatre of the mind. And even though they act in many "plays" and play many "parts," they know the starring role goes to the one who practices and rehearses more often and more effectively than anyone else. When you mix theories with the right amount of rehearsed action, they will come to life on a stage everyone else will see. This is when you get practical and when it gets real.

What about you? Do you value experimentation and practice as much as you should? If yes, why do you believe this is good for you and others? If not, what will you do to change?

The UNCOMMODiFiED demonstrate a relentless desire to practice the skills and behaviours that take their ideas from their minds into the real world. They rehearse, practice, live out their theories, and flesh them out with others. This inspires people to value, as they do, the private work of practice and the public work of performance and experimentation. Beyond entertaining flights of fancy or unproven wishful thinking, transformation in the real world comes from the practical power of hope-filled action.

Thirdly, the Unequivocally Practical are generators, not just Generals. They focus their practical power on both generating valuable ideas and generating the energy required to make those ideas useful in the real world. They refuse to use their position and power to command or demand. Instead, they command your attention with their down-to-earth, practical approach to everything. They understand that once you crystallize an idea in someone's mind, you must catalyze their focus and infuse energy to bring it to life. Being practical is hard work. But when you energize and encourage people, they will work harder and go further without burning out along the way.

Lastly, UNCOMMODiFiED practical people who inspire the most have street smarts, not just book smarts. Whether they have degrees after their name or no formal education, they all have street smarts. It is what keeps them from getting lost in heady ideas and ideals and allows them to find simple actions to make real what they dream. They are both daydreamers and daring doers.

> **THE UNCOMMODIFIED ARE SEERS AND DOERS, PRACTICAL PROPHETS, AND WISE WANDERERS.**

They understand what it takes to make it in the real world and what it takes to realize their dreams. They refuse to leave good ideas on pages or in their heads. Instead, they take what they learn and what they can imagine and work it out in life. As Scottish author and government reformer Samuel Miles wrote, "Practical wisdom is only to be learned in the school of experience."[71] And I would add, "and the school of hard knocks." The most inspiring and influential people I know have received their practical wisdom from these schools. They inspire others to take thoughts, ideas and inspirations and write their own story, running towards what they want to see and do. They are seers and doers, practical prophets, and wise wanderers.

So, now it's time for you to get out of your head, out of the clouds of theory and into your real world. It's time to get unequivocally practical. It's time to create and catalyze the attention and energy required to make "practical magic" and inspire "practical action." It's time to let your ideas ooze robust usability and usefulness.

UNCAGE iT... NOW!

Do you create and catalyze enough attention from others to inspire the practical action required to succeed? If not, how will you make sure you do that more effectively?

How do you create and catalyze enough energy from others to inspire the practical action required to succeed?

How can you make your ideas and theories more usable and useful? Think of three things you can do differently and better to do this.

NUMBER TEN ...
My mentors are so UNDERSTANDABLY PLAINSPOKEN that they even come through loud and clear to the hard of hearing.

The practical magic of the UNCOMMODiFiED is empowered by their innate ability to make things simple, easily understood, and actionable. Their desire and ability to be understandably plainspoken is transformational.

They blow off the "fog" with their plainspokenness, and that helps people see clearer and move faster. Think about it, if you're driving down a country road and hit a thick fog bank, you immediately slow down and get fearful. And this is what happens when you are not understandably plainspoken. People's productivity and performance are impeded. And that's why UNCOMMODiFiED people make it their goal to blow the fog off the road, so those journeying with them stay on course and move toward their shared goal at highway speed.

> **How about you? Are you a fog reducer or a fog producer? Does your communication burn off the "fog" for you and others? Can people clearly see the future and the pathway?**

When the Understandably Plainspoken explain something to you, you simply get it. When they are pleased with your performance, you know it. When disappointed in your performance, they clearly articulate what changes they would like to see you make, for your sake and theirs.

Here are some plainspoken DON'TS and DO'S I have gleaned from my UNCOMMODiFiED tutors over the years. If we heed this advice, you and I will become as understandably plainspoken as they are.

Don't avoid the main point of what you want to say.
Get to it. And maybe repeat it. Often, we cloud what we want to communicate with unnecessary information and ideas. And that's a problem, which leads to my second point.

Don't speak in a roundabout or indirect way.
Just say it. Having good intentions to be clear does not mean you create understanding when you skirt around the issue and are ambiguous in your delivery.

and, Don't use jargon.
Please, don't! Jargon is the words or expressions used only by specific industries, professions, groups, or classes of people. Jargon is complicated for other people to understand. It might be your language but not theirs, so your jargon is the enemy of being clearly understood.

I recently came across a fascinating website launched in 1994 that speaks to this point. It's called *plainlanguage.gov*,[72] created by the *Plain Language Action and Information Network,* a working group of American federal employees who support clear communication in government writing.

It might sound like an oxymoron or a great comedy sketch: "clear communication from the government." But the goal of this group is to promote the use of plain language in all government communications. They believe communicating in simple language will save federal agencies time and money and provide better service to the American public.

Here's what they encourage on their website: "Speak plainly … When you're making word choices, pick the familiar or commonly used word over the unusual or obscure."

So, avoid using jargon, unnecessarily complicated terms, and unfamiliar acronyms unless you prefer to try to impress your audience rather than inform them. This is extremely important if you want to be more understandably plainspoken.

Do speak directly and honestly.
Be truthful and straightforward. Be blunt AND kind. And while this may seem like a contradiction, it is not. It is what people want and need from you.

Do become the simple synonyms of the word *plainspoken*:
Candid, direct, frank, honest, open, plain, and upfront.[73] People will more easily understand what you are saying.

and, Do speak their language.
In episode #14 of the UNCOMMODiFiED Podcast, I talked with my friend Craig Minchin who said MLK essentially spoke in "tongues." Now that is interesting, but what does it mean? Well, it's relatively simple. He spoke the language of the people he wanted to communicate clearly with, whether they were politicians, marginalized people, or priests. He was understandably plainspoken. No matter whom he was speaking to, he spoke their language. If they were Black or White, it didn't matter; he could speak their language. Rich or Poor, it didn't matter; he could speak their language. And that's what made him such a great communicator.

Here's my simple, plainspoken challenge: make your ideas and instructions easy to understand and act on. Get understandably plainspoken — it is what everyone needs from you today.

UNCAGE iT... NOW!

When you communicate, do you make ideas and instructions simple to understand and easy to act on? If so, why do you believe you're great at this? And if not, how are you going to do this more effectively?

What jargon, and what unnecessarily complicated language, terms, or acronyms do you need to stop using so your communication will be more understandable?

Do you value being candid, direct, frank, honest, open, plain, and upfront with people? If so, why do you believe this is good for you and them? And if not, how will you explore the value of this behaviour?

NUMBER ELEVEN ...
They are silver-tongued angels, UNRIVALED "PAINTERS" who can help you feel the heaven in your hell.

My UNCOMMODiFiED mentors have provoked me to become a PAINTER WHO PAINTS inspirational visions of the future as they do, like Dr. Kevin, who runs a medical clinic in rural Zimbabwe. When I first met him, he spoke so passionately and "painted" such an enticing vision of transforming the government officials in his community into advocates and allies, not adversaries of the local villagers. When Dr. Kevin "painted" this possibility in my mind, somehow, I "saw" the powerful impact we could have as if it was already done – leaders leading for the sake of their people. I listened and "saw" it with my "heart" and was compelled to partner with him. Over the years, his "painting" became our reality as we had the privilege of conducting leadership training that positively impacted the region's most influential political leaders and bureaucrats.

Inspired by masters like Dr. Kevin, MLK and Winston Churchill, though not at their level, I have become a "painter" too. Not with an easel or acrylic paints, not with a brush or palate. But with the tonality of my voice and words flowing from typing fingers, I now PAINT with the "figurative language" of ==metaphors, similes, analogies,== and ==allegories.== And you can, too. In fact, take an "art" lesson right now from the "master of metaphors" himself. Watch MLK's "I have a dream" speech on YouTube[74] and get inspired.

Let's explore this idea: "painting" with **metaphors**. It's time to get below the surface of "just the facts" communication, slip behind the curtain and begin to see how the neuroscience of metaphors can work in your favour. To ensure we're all on the same page, let's look at a simple definition of a metaphor: "A poetic or crafty way of saying one thing is something else to emphasize a point or create a strong reaction or feeling."[75] I used an example earlier in this chapter when I said the most inspiring and influential people are "fire starters and stokers." I assume you understood I wasn't calling them arsonists or encouraging you to be one. I was saying something much more provocative. Metaphors powerfully convey significant truths in minimal time and space. Metaphors speak the language of the brain and the emotions, which is why they are powerful literary and communication devices.

Here's how neuroscience works when it comes to metaphors. Your brain is constantly scanning for connections, patterns and meaning. So it sees and interprets literal and metaphoric ideas in almost the same way. When your brain makes an association between the literal and the metaphoric, it sends messages to your body, triggering associated sensations. Try this: "Suddenly, she had an idea that set her brain on fire." Metaphors like this allow us to experience ideas viscerally. Powerfully. This is why metaphors are so brilliant for helping us express ideas and create powerfully associated feelings. In fMRI experiments, neuroscientists discovered that expressions like "That caused a hairy situation for us" lit up brain areas associated with touch and feel.[76] Fascinating. Interestingly, literal, non-metaphoric approaches to communicating the same information do not stimulate those areas of the brain.

So, if you want people to "feel" what you're saying and be moved because of it, "paint" with metaphors and unleash their power.

You can also "paint" with **similes**: a simile compares one thing to another in order to compare traits together in a compelling way. This catalyzes and crystalizes attention and allows for comparative understanding. Here's an example of a powerful simile: "To win this fight, you must be as brave as a lion."

We know this simile evokes something more than just run-of-the-mill courage. We're talking about "lion-like" courage. I should know. I remember feeding lions and walking among them during my time in Africa, and I feel the power of those incredible creatures whenever I come across this simile.

You can "paint" with **analogies**: an analogy highlights a shared characteristic for emphasis, like the famous example from the movie Forrest Gump: "Life is like a box of chocolates. You never know what you're going to get."[77] This analogy suggests that life has many choices and surprises, just like a box of chocolates. Once the connection is made, once it's painted with your tongue and vocal inflection, people will feel it and be moved by it and might even want to eat chocolate.

"Once mastered, people will be compelled by the unrivalled visions you evoke in their minds using nothing more than words."

Finally, you can also "brush" your communication with **allegories**: allegories are stories, poems, or pictures that reveal a hidden meaning. Like the parables that great teachers like Jesus used to make the mysterious "sacred," just simple everyday truths that even children could understand. Like the ancient Greek myth of Icarus and Daedalus.[78] Icarus's father, Daedalus, fashioned wings made of wax, so his son could escape imprisonment. But in his arrogance, Icarus flew too close to the sun, his wings melted, and he fell into the sea and drowned. Clearly, this story has a message. As an allegory, it may caution us about the dangers of reaching too far beyond our powers and the consequences of overambition. This allegory, once artfully painted with words, once conveyed with tongue and inflection, allows people to feel the sun's heat and be moved to keep their wings far from it. Or, better yet, perhaps the allegory causes them to consider making heat-resistant wings!

Once mastered, people will be compelled by the unrivalled visions you evoke in their minds using nothing more than words. It's time for you to become an Unrivalled PAINTER. Here's my challenge: dip your tongue (or pen) in "silver paint" and become a "silver-tongued" angel. Paint with concrete images that make comparisons to enhance your communication. Paint with metaphors, similes, analogies, allegories, and any other figurative language you can imagine. Paint so powerfully on the canvas of people's minds and hearts that you inspire and positively influence them toward a brighter future: a brighter future so tangible that when you paint it for them, they can see it, touch it, and taste it.

UNCAGE iT... NOW!

```
Are you great at painting with metaphors and
similes? If so, why do you believe you're great
at this? And if not, how will you explore these
powerful literary devices this week?

Are you great at painting with analogies? If so,
why do you believe you're great at this? And if
not, how will you explore these powerful literary
devices this week?

Are you great at painting with allegories? If so,
why do you believe you're great at this? And if
not, how will you explore these powerful literary
devices this week?
```

NUMBER TWELVE …
The UNCOMMODiFiED are so UNAPOLOGETICALLY PROVOCATIVE you may find yourself thanking them for pissing you off enough to get you off your ass and into the arena.

We've come to the final characteristic that makes my UNCOMMODiFiED tutors, and hopefully me and you along with them, uncommonly inspirational and influential.

They say whatever happens in Vegas stays in Vegas. I'm here to call bullshit by "kissing and telling". I was in Sin City on a business trip when a client came up with a superhero name for me: "Agent Provocateur." I love it and own it. It's become one of my favourite nicknames ever bestowed on me. Over the years, it continues to resonate. I believe it is both a compliment and a confirmation of what I endeavour to do every time I partner with people in their personal and professional development.

Let me tell you a quick story that helps illustrate my training and coaching philosophy. Years ago, I developed a sore shoulder that persisted and was not improving. So, I went to my chiropractor, who diagnosed it as bursitis, loosely meaning "a nagging pain that won't go away." When I first saw him, he said my shoulder wasn't injured enough for my body to do anything about it, which was why the pain persisted. So, he performed deep tissue massage, which aggravated the muscle a bit more. He said this approach would cause my body to recognize and treat it as a problem. It would take a bit of time, about three weeks, but he promised that it would get better. And, sure enough, it did.

This experience has become a metaphor for my training and coaching philosophy. ==I endeavour to "hurt" you and cause just enough "pain" to get your attention and energy focused on what==

==you need to change or learn.== If I can be a "provocateur of discomfort," maybe you will feel enough "pain" and want to change and grow. It may sound unorthodox, but it works.

The word *"provocative"* means "causing annoyance, anger or strong reaction."[79] That's me. I cause annoyance, anger, and strong reaction. It is what I do and what I do best. I do it deliberately. I do it on purpose, like my chiropractor did when he wounded me so I could heal. And the most UNCOMMODiFiED people I have had the privilege to meet and work with have done it to me as well. They do provocative things on purpose. They annoy you, even make you angry, create a strong reaction, and provoke you to do or be something different or better. The unapologetically provocative fulfill, with an almost "holy" aggression, a mandate found in a New Testament book called Hebrews: "Let us consider how we may provoke one another on toward love and good deeds."[80] One translation even uses the word SPUR in place of the word provoke.

Here's how I interpret this mandate: I'll get on your back and drive my spurs deep into your sides to motivate you towards something better, for your sake and others. I will provoke, push, poke and prod you with my well-chosen words and well-crafted questions in the direction of the actions you and others must take to catalyze change.

And at the end of the day, this is what being UNCOMMODiFiED is all about for me. Provocative people are edgy, inciting, incendiary and instigating.[81] __They are fire starters and stokers, and I am all of this and more on some days.__

The UNCOMMODiFiED are persuasive provocateurs. They are rabble-rousers. They are magicians. And when they work their magic, they transform right before your eyes from provocateur to evocator: an inspiring, influential sage who conjures up spirits;[82] a provocative person who calls your soul from the dead and breathes new life into your purpose and destiny.

Let's get unapologetically provocative right now. Let's challenge ourselves to become provocateurs, even evocators. Buy a ticket for your inner Agent Provocateur and your Agent Evocator and fly home from Vegas. Get on the back of anyone who will invite you to drive your spurs deep into their side and motivate them towards greater love and more wondrous good deeds for the primary benefit of others.

UNCAGE iT... NOW!

What will you do to release your "Agent Provocateur" and your inner "Agent Evocative" to positively inspire and influence others?

Who needs you to "spur" them on this week toward their better future and destiny? How and when will you do this?

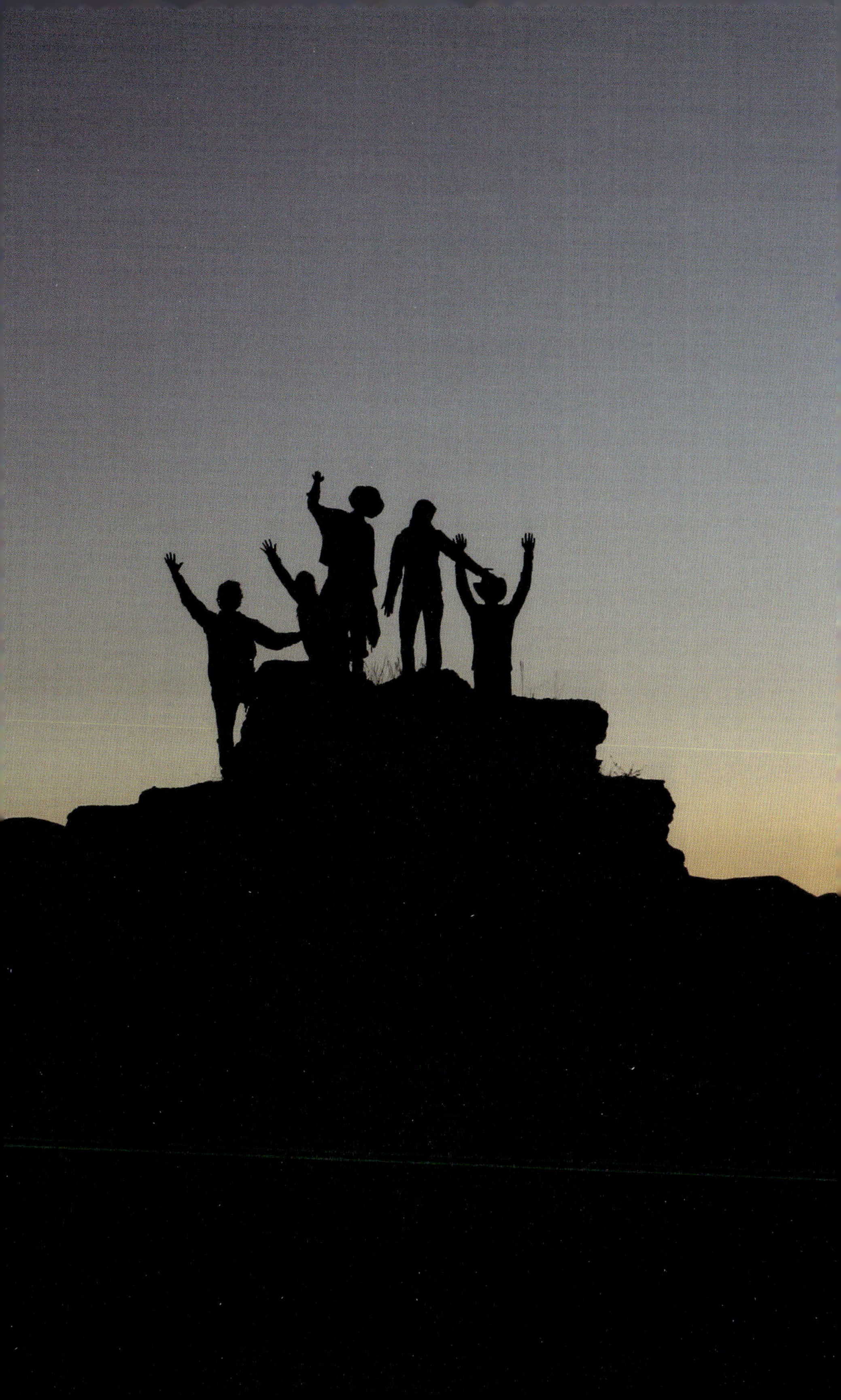

the UNCOMMODiFieD are UNDETERRED and UNDENIED

This is the chapter that will give you the chutzpah to keep on going ... and going.

6

YOU CAN'T STOP the UNCOMMODiFiED. You can't push them down, and you can't pull them back. They won't let you or any force of nature deny them the fulfillment of their predetermined and possibly predestined future. Come hell or high water, raging seas, diabolical demons (theirs or yours), they will get there, preferably with you, but even without you, if that's what it takes. They have unusual rigour and will ultimately be rewarded, even if the reward is subtly or substantially different than expected.

UNCOMMODiFiED people are consistently undeterred and undenied from their destinies. The dictionary defines "undeterred" this way: "They are not discouraged or prevented from acting."[83] Criticism or problems do not rattle them. As Babe Ruth said, "It's hard to beat a person who never gives up."[84]

The UNCOMMODiFiED are also "undenied" and, therefore, undeniable. They won't be denied, so they live by the mantra: "Yes, I can. Yes, I will. Yes, I must." They get shit done and make shit happen. They are genuine and know where they want to go and who they want to become. They have a plan and a process to get them there. Instead of just meeting expectations, they consistently outperform everyones' expectations.

You've probably heard of the 80/20 principle:[85] the theory that 80% of outcomes (or outputs) result from 20% of all causes (or inputs). I like to express it this way ... **it is the 20 percent of the vital few things we do that produce 80 percent of the results we achieve.** So, I prefer to call it the 20/80 principle. The undeterred and undenied are 20/80 people. Their consistent micro actions fuel their macro results. They know how to move the fulcrum and push the lever. Archimedes said, "Give me a lever long enough and a fulcrum on which to place it, and I shall move the world."[86] The undeterred and undenied know what levers to push, what fulcrums to build and to move, and this guarantees them a more effective push towards their predetermined outcomes, the things they want to and plan to achieve.

The UNCOMMODiFiED are story writers and storytellers. Let me paint a picture of some inspiring Zimbabweans; Peter, Scott, Brian, and Lance, who created fertile farms by pressing their hands deep into the dry soil. These UNCOMMODiFiED changemakers built dams and gave a damn. They taught people to feed themselves, their families, and their friends. They transformed the world around them, even when their lives got difficult. Though nature and politics often conspired against them, they did not shrink from the outcome they sought but remained undeterred and undenied.

Remember my friend Harmon? He's the bridge builder and CNN hero who, along with his Bridging the Gap Africa team, builds bridges to a better life in the walking world, positively impacting entire communities in rural Kenya. Even when massive floods washed away many of their bridges, the team remained steadfast and began to rebuild them. They didn't give up, and they don't give in. If you want to learn more about Harmon and his passion for "bridging the gap," you can listen to episode #23 of the UNCOMMODiFiED Podcast.

In Mozambique, I worked with a formidable woman named Tracy, the physician assistant I referred to in the last chapter. When I first met her, she rode horseback through the rural countryside, providing health care, undeterred by the absence of safe roads or shelters. Then there's Julie, who sat beneath a tree with me and some village elders, sharing her vision to set up a school system to bring better education to rural village children. Both she and Tracy were undeterred and undenied in improving education and healthcare.

> "All of them had dreams. Some saw them fulfilled in their lifetime, while others saw them fulfilled from beyond the veil of their mortality. Yet, even still, they remained undeterred and undenied."

Here are a few other people from history who never gave up:[87] JK Rowling, whose Harry Potter debut novel was rejected by twelve publishers; Nelson Mandela, who, from within his jail cell, helped bring about an end to South African apartheid; and MLK, the civil rights champion who positively impacted race relations around the world even though he died before the age of 40. None of them flinched from what they wanted to accomplish. Look at their biographies and read the stories of how they made the impossible possible. All of them had dreams. Some saw them fulfilled in their lifetime, while others saw them fulfilled from beyond the veil of their mortality. Their stories inspire us to press in and press on.

Consider my friend, Norm, who lost his wife to cancer. Norm owned two engineering companies, which he sold off, along with his beautiful home on the shore of Lake Ontario in Canada. He developed a deep desire to create a meaningful, impactful community around him, so instead of retiring in lavish obscurity, he funded the construction of a six-story apartment building in which he had a one-bedroom unit. Norm fulfilled his vision with the help of others and created a place of genuine community. He didn't let himself be thwarted or denied. Encouraging me to get involved, we, along with others, spearheaded an unusual, UNCOMMODiFiED food bank experience. It functioned more like a store, with prices on donated items, but you couldn't buy them with cash. People who needed help were dignified with the opportunity to "shop" in the store and choose what they liked instead of receiving just what someone handed to them. That apartment building remains a center of community hope, healing, and connectivity. And even though Norm is no longer there (he died years ago), his impact survives because he remained undeterred and undenied in fulfilling his vision.

When I look at the lives of all these people, I ask myself, what makes the UNCOMMODiFiED so undeterred and undenied? What qualities do they possess? After many years of pondering this question, I have culled a list of twelve positive predispositions, twelve rigorous characteristics that mark the undeterred and undenied people I have met. And if you and I can possess and practice them, we can and will become as undeterred and undenied as they are.

The UNCOMMODiFiED are LONG HAULERS.

Long-haul truck drivers don't just drive a day route. They drive a long way every day. They understand the journey is long and the road is winding. The pathway to success is never a straight highway. And because they know there are no shortcuts in life, they sustain themselves and others with their ability to drive on even when the sun is setting. Long haulers maintain their "vehicles," balance their "load," and make sure they and others have enough emotional and physical "fuel" for the journey.

"Long Haulers" also know that sometimes the journey will require them to get out of the truck and walk or even run to their destination. They understand that life is a marathon, not a sprint, and they run and fuel appropriately, and we must do this as well. It will take a prolonged and sometimes challenging effort to accomplish the things we want. This is called endurance, and there's no shortcut. We must take the long way, the long road, if we want to create a lasting impact. To live by this wise principle, you must dig deep and develop the endurance required to reach your destination. Like our friend, Dorothy, who my wife and I chatted with in her living room just months before she died in her mid-90s. Dorothy was a "long hauler." I remember, with great affection, the joy she recounted of seeing many of the dreams she had for her spiritual community realized over her lifetime. Some of those dreams took years, and some took decades to find their fulfillment. And this, she said, gave her complete confidence that the dreams she still desired to see would be realized after she was gone.

Living "long haul" is a hallmark of the UNCOMMODiFiED. Long days. Long nights. Early mornings. All laser-focused on creating long-lasting impact. Some live many years, some not enough years, but all live all the days they have to their fullest.

> **So, ask yourself:**
> # DO YOU LIVE LONG HAUL?
> # ARE YOU A MARATHONER?
> # OR ARE YOU A SPRINTER?

They are TENACIOUSLY PATIENT.

The dictionary defines tenacious as "not easily pulled apart; cohesive; adhering to or clinging to; persistent in seeking something of value or desire."[88]

The undeterred and undenied people I have met were tenaciously patient. They manifested aggressive forbearance. They were not hasty, not always in a mad rush, AND, not BUT, AND they were persistent and tenacious. There was a tenacity, a ferocity in their patience. Now, that may sound like an oxymoron, but mixing these two paradoxical traits is the alchemy of their success.

My UNCOMMODiFiED, tenaciously patient friends have a unique ability to abide in this tension, much like teams do in a tug of war: pulling to hold the flag on the rope in the middle. This tension creates a powerful and provocative balance, a push and pull that ultimately makes them undeterred and undenied people who allow this powerful push and pull to propel them and others forward.

Like the farmers I partnered with in rural Zimbabwe, they have a hurry-up-and-wait mentality. First, they work furiously to prepare their fields and push the seed deep into the ground, and then the waiting begins. They patiently wait for the rains to come and the sun to shine, all the while closely monitoring the growth and maturity of the crop.

How about you? Are you tenacious and patient? Are you tenacious and not patient enough? Or are you patient but not aggressive enough? What have you suffered long for? What is required today to soothe that suffering: more tenacity or more patience?

The UNCOMMODiFiED FALL FORWARD.

They resist the pull and temptation to fall backwards. Rather than falling on their ass and getting discouraged when they fail, they fall forward. Falling forward enables momentum to be regained and sustained. Failures catalyze their attention, and they learn from their own mistakes and the mistakes of others instead of being crushed by them. They fail upward and fall forward.

I've witnessed this in my undeterred and undenied tutors countless times. When their plans got thwarted, they just made new ones. When the rains washed away their buildings and bridges, they built them again. When drought literally and figuratively tried to strangle the life and hope out of them and others, they found new ways to irrigate the land and their hearts. And, of course, they repeatedly fell and failed. But each time, they rolled with the punches and brushed the dust off as they sprang back onto their feet with renewed passion and even more persistence.

What about you? Do you fall face forward? Or do you fall ass backwards when failure or discouragement comes your way? Do you recoil? Or do you fall forward and press into the learning required to possess what you desire?

They LEAN into LEARNING.

The UNCOMMODiFiED lean into experimentation and learning; they are "alchemists" who test their theories in the real world, making their "magic" very practical. They are undeterred and undenied because they squeeze new ideas and information out of their experiences in order to make better decisions in the future. For them, difficulty is like smelling salts, that awakens the brilliance within them. We must never forget that the challenges we encounter energize the genius of thinking new ideas.

> "They learn new ideas and ancient wisdom to save themselves and others from the predictable problems that come when we do not learn from history and prepare ourselves for the future."

They love learning at the library. They're always reading something. They buy (and actually read) the newest and oldest books to gain the practical wisdom required to ensure that they and others will be undeterred and undenied in every endeavour. They explore new ideas and learn ancient wisdom to save themselves and others from the predictable problems that come when we do not learn from history and prepare ourselves for the future.

When I think of this quality, I see and hear my son Chris. For many years books were just things that his Mom, Dad, or Teachers recommended and read. But not now. He loves to read and leans hard into learning, experimentation, and testing. As a senior leader in a mid-size corporation, he is unafraid to tell everyone he is on a learning journey and to invite them to join. Over the past years, he has "made" me read many books and has given me the privilege of partnering with him in using their core principles to provoke the thinking of his team. He continually seeks ideas and strategies that confirm and confront his beliefs and behaviours. He leans into learning that will help him and others learn from the mistakes of others, evolve, stay ahead of their competition and serve their customers. I am continually inspired by his ability to be agile and to hold the truth he passionately believes today openhandedly. His willingness to shift directions, twist, and turn in response to an insightful new idea that he read on yet another plane ride is a powerful model to emulate. I have such deep respect for his curious nature, and I live and will die proud and confident that he will always be an UNCOMMODiFiED man who will be undeterred and undenied in all his quests.

> The UNCOMMODiFiED also love to learn from the lives of others.

They're always reading someone else's mind. They seek mentors and tutors who will impart the time-tested wisdom that only real-life experiments, experience, and testing can teach. They lean into the learning that others have already discovered, borrow that wisdom, and put it to work for them.

Do you lean into learning? What's the last book you read, and what did it teach you? Who is the last sage you sat with, and what did you learn from them? Does difficulty wake up the genius in you? Or does difficulty crush you, causing you to recoil and sit on the floor in a fetal position?

The UNCOMMODiFiED are ENERGIZED BY FEAR.

I want to be clear: the UNCOMMODiFiED get afraid, scared and even terrified. Of course, they have insecurities and are fearful of things. But it's what they do with that fear that makes them so UNCOMMODiFiED. They constantly challenge themselves and others to turn the negative energy of their fears into positive forward momentum. They know that being brutally honest with themselves and others about what scares the shit out of them is the only way to break free from those fears.

> *"They know that being brutally honest with themselves and others about what scares the shit out of them is the only way to break free from those fears."*

Pretending we are not afraid in a bid to build the confidence of others is an unwise strategy. People see right through that and will see right through you. The terror in your soul is displayed on your face and heard in your voice. But here's the secret: we are actually energized by our fears when we face them head-on. When we allow others to see us honestly engage our fears, they see that we are just like them, humans who get afraid, but we also demonstrate that we do not need to be paralyzed by those fears. And, as my UNCOMMODiFiED mentors constantly remind me, statistically 91.4% of what we fear and worry about will never happen.

Here's another lesson I have learned. You will never eliminate all the fear, so you must "do it scared." If you get past the fear, you will find the rush. Remember, baby steps. The first step is the hardest. Focus on where you are. Get your eyes on something inspiring and just do it. It will get easier.

If you want to let your fears energize you, listen to episode #77 of the UNCOMMODiFiED Podcast, entitled *"BLOW YOUR FEARS AWAY: the Secret Power of Your Nervous Farts."* In this UNCORK Conversation, Natasha McKenty (media specialist, television broadcaster, news writer, and FEAR FACER) and I explore our terrors and tears. Natasha shares her personal and professional journey from being terrified of crowds and speaking in public to being in front of crowds and the camera and "going public" for the sake of others.

> Now it's your turn.
> Be energized by your fears and use them to move you forward.

They are AGGRESSIVE ANTAGONISTS.

The UNCOMMODiFiED wage war against the status quo. The Latin meaning of status quo is "the state in which we find things."[89] My undeterred and undenied mates are not happy with the way things are. Instead of leaving things in the state in which they find them, they seek to improve them, like my friends Peter, Scott, Brian, Lance, Harmon, Paul, Tracy, Julie, Norm and others you have already met in this book. They are and were aggressive antagonists who made a past-time of picking a fight with the status quo. I recall one experience I had with Tracy as she gently, yet forcefully held the outstretched hand of a Mozambiquan police officer who wanted to extort a bribe from her on the side of the road. She was not going to pay the "fine" and go with the flow, the status quo of corruption. She drove away that day and on many other occasions with the same amount of money in her pocket as when he had stopped her. She peacefully drove away from these scenarios as an aggressive antagonist of a desperately corrupt system.

One of the greatest gifts I have received from observing my UNCOMMODiFiED aggressive antagonists is the assurance that the power of injustice can be shattered. The status quo is not invincible. They remind me that small acts of kindness are not insignificant but potentially transformational. Don't be deceived or deceive yourself. When many of us do nothing, then nothing is done. And when many of us do nothing, absolutely nothing changes. The status quo, "the way things are," requires that no one makes a peep. So, get noisy. Get aggressively antagonistic.

> **WHAT DO YOU THINK?**
>
> **ARE YOU AN <u>AGGRESSIVE ANTAGONIST</u>?**
>
> **DO YOU PUT UP WITH THE STATUS QUO?**
>
> **DO YOU THROW YOUR HANDS UP IN DEFEAT AND SAY THERE'S NOTHING YOU CAN DO?**
>
> **DO YOU PRESS IN AND DO SOMETHING ABOUT IT WITH POSITIVE AGGRESSION?**

They live OUTSTRETCHED, not CRUNCHED UP.

The UNCOMMODiFiED live with outstretched hands. They are not miserly and do not fear suffering a sense of loss when they freely give what they have to others. Living large, expanding lives, they're always reaching out, reaching into and reaching further. The "outstretched" are generous with their personal resources, time, and relational connections.

After recently recording a podcast episode with my friend Craig, we sat in my backyard and shared a wee dram of Scotch and a cigar. As we chatted about life and the values we desire to demonstrate, Craig asked who influenced me most in shaping my generosity, my sense of living outstretched, not crunched up. As I sipped my drink and reflected on his questions, I realized, again, it was my mom. She taught me to live generously, with an open-handedness to those around me. Even when we didn't have very much, she always gave freely. As a young boy, I can remember being allowed to volunteer with my mom at a senior's home in our community. She didn't demand that I serve others. Instead, she showed me why it was meaningful and invited me to do it with her. She always had her hand outstretched with generosity and encouraged and inspired me to do the same.

==In 2013 an "outstretched, not crunched up" force of nature joined our family.== My UNCOMMODiFiED daughter-in-law Emily is gregarious by nature and generous by nurture (thanks to her parents) with her time, attention, and deep appreciation for everyone. Emily lives impressively available to her neighbours, nieces, co-workers and even the odd stray cat. Open-house and open-handed are the way she rolls. Her "drop over anytime" and "We have people coming to dinner again tonight; do you guys want to come too?" texts and calls are breathtaking. No, really, it exhausts me just thinking about all the food to be prepped and dishes to wash. But not Emily; she is invigorated by it all. She lives inspirationally "uncrunched" — open to others. Her ability to create community with other humans is amazing, and she challenges me to up my "community building" game every day. Emily is, and I am most confident she always will be, undeterred and undenied in her quest to make everyone she encounters feel valued and loved.

How about you? Do you live outstretched? Or do you clutch onto what you have because you're scared it won't ever come back if you give it away?

The UNCOMMODiFiED BACK UP, not DOWN.

Obstacles provide opportunities to back up, regroup, refocus, and find a different route. And just the right sort and measure of stubbornness keeps us moving forward and upward.

The UNCOMMODiFiED don't back down from any fight. Time and time again, I have gone to battle alongside my undeterred and undenied friends in pursuit of what we intrinsically know is "right," not a selfish or self-serving cause that makes us look vital, but those moments when we know the greater good is at stake. I remember standing on the "battlefield" with Peter in Zimbabwe, standing up to injustice and standing with rural villagers harassed by the authorities. Peter told me, "We can choose to take one step back, but we must never back down and let injustice crush them and us." Those words still provoke and inspire me today.

"MAYBE YOU JUST NEED TO BACK UP NOT BACK DOWN FROM THE ADVERSITY THAT'S TRYING TO KEEP YOU FROM REALIZING YOUR GOAL"

Listen to the wisdom of these two inspiring men who backed up but not down. Henry Ford said, "Failure is the opportunity to begin again, this time more intelligently."[90] Thomas Edison said, "Our greatest weakness lies in giving up. The most certain way to succeed is always to try just one more time."[91] And he also said, "Many of life's failures are people who did not realize how close they were to success when they gave up."[92]

Maybe you just need to back up, not back down, from the adversity that's trying to keep you from realizing your goal. That's what being undeterred and undenied is all about.

So, how about you? Are you backing up or backing down from a problem getting in the way of what you want to achieve?

They SIT and STAY in the PAIN.

Einstein said of himself: "I'm not so smart. It's just that I stay with problems longer."[93] That's a powerful way of living, being willing to stay and maybe even suffer a little as we consider the problem we seek to solve.

Staying in the pain of the problem long enough for it to be a provocation is an identifying characteristic of the UNCOMMODiFiED. They don't resist or run away from pain. Instead, by converting negative experiences into positive energy, they fuel momentum and understand that the "phoenix" must be engulfed in flames to emerge renewed. Like a phoenix, undeterred and undenied people burn and emerge better, stronger. They burn with passion, bearing the pain of others, their cultures, and societies. The burning causes them to emerge triumphant because they've stayed in it long enough. They do not recoil from pain but allow it to be a provocation.

Here's what I have gleaned by watching my UNCOMMODiFiED gurus: sitting in the pain is also cathartic and catalytic. We need the discomfort to grow sufficient dissatisfaction in us and in others to compel us to action. If we are not utterly dissatisfied, we will not fight for transformation. If we remove ourselves from the place that pains us too quickly, we will go away bruised but not burned. And it's only when our hearts are burned and broken that we are compelled to live with vulnerability, awake to the pain we must feel and soothe.

In my late 30s, I experienced a profound lesson about learning to sit and stay in the pain long enough for it to become a provocation.

This is when I first met Patrice, a woman who suffered debilitating schizophrenia and spent years living in the psychiatric ward of our local hospital. Patrice became a good friend of our family during this time, and we spent countless hours listening to her horrific life story. As she recounted the excruciating pain of her childhood and present life, her pain became mine. I was deeply grieved for her and angered by how people had taken advantage of her over the years. The more I sat with her in her pain, the more motivated I became to help. As a result, we partnered with Patrice for years serving her friends and neighbours. When Patrice's landlord (and a friend of mine at the time) tried to have her evicted, I went with her to a rental tribunal eviction hearing and successfully represented her so she could remain in her home. I was, on that day, just a man who chose to sit and stay in the pain of another person's story long enough for it to provoke me to uncomfortable and relentless action.

So, here's my question: Do you stay in the pain of the problem long enough, or do you run away from it?

The UNCOMMODiFiED are ELASTIC.

If you want to be undeterred, you need to be able to stretch without snapping, as my UNCOMMODiFiED mentors do. They don't break. They're not brittle, but instead, they are strengthened by struggle. If you shake them, they just get stronger and more resolved.[94] There is an elasticity to them. You can stretch and bend them, but they won't break.

In difficult times, they morph, flex, and adjust to the constraints of the environment they find themselves in. They have the unique ability to thrive and become more useful when they are stretched beyond their perceived limits. Imagine a box of wine glasses. You could make it more resistant to breaking by padding the box more. But what if the glasses could become more robust each time you try to break them?[95] That is what these undeterred and undenied people are like.

Meet my friend Terry; he's a truly UNCOMMODiFiED, elastic "cool cat" with way more than nine lives. When circumstances try to shake and shatter him, they just make him stronger. Since the day I met Terry, he has been an exemplar of this innate birthright. From the time he was a young boy, he was already in training to live an "elastic" life. Everyone tried to shatter his dreams, but they could not. His dreams and the dreamer within him just got bigger and bolder. Whatever he dreamed he could do, he did it. Born in a rustic world where art and creativity were seen as a waste of time and talent, he thumbed his nose and said "fuck you" to his naysayers. He became a filmmaker, painter, and artist whose work over the past four decades is now owned by collectors on four continents. But don't think life has gotten easy for Terry over the years because it hasn't. I walked with him as a friend and fan as he endured catastrophic shaking when one million dollars was embezzled from him and his beautiful studio on a forested pond and waterfall adorned oasis was seized. This event would have destroyed most people, but not Terry. At the time I am writing this, the most extraordinary creative work he has ever undertaken still hangs in the balance between death and life. His grand cinematic and dramatic artwork dream, which he has passionately pursued for many years, is still in the shaking stage. But, as with all of Terry's dreams, I am thoroughly convinced that this one will also be fully birthed from his soul into the real world for all of us to enjoy with our eyes, ears, and hearts.

What about you? Are you fragile or unbreakable? Are you elastic or brittle? The ability to snap back after being stretched beyond our limits is a real challenge for all of us. It isn't easy to stay intact when difficult things come our way. But if we break, we will be denied. If we are shattered, we won't find our ultimate success.

They remain PURPOSELY NAÏVE.

Are you naïve enough to believe? Are you childlike but not childish: wide eyed and curious yet not immature? Choose, and it is a choice, to perceive the world with childlike wonder. Untainted by cynicism in all your endeavours, this is the way of the undeterred and undenied.

> "The problem is some of us ADULT way too much."

I see in my grandchildren this beautiful naivety, this unbridled possibility. Since they haven't yet experienced much real disappointment, their options remain positive, endless, and vast, and I'm convinced this is how we all should live. The problem is some of us "adult" way too much.

I have also seen this characteristic of playful openness in my UNCOMMODiFiED provocateurs. This ability is both spectacular and captivating. It is an ability to invite others to dream like a wide-eyed child who still believes that the "red-suited man" can get down the chimney you don't have. My "adulting" seems to lose its capacity to limit my imagination and creativity when I am in my grandkids' presence. I am a "child" again, and my newfound naivety allows me to play make-believe games like I did when I was young. Back then, I could be anyone I wanted to be. My imagination could overcome my circumstances. My fatherlessness or our financial problems didn't limit me. I was an explorer like Indiana Jones. And the truth is that I can be one right now, again, if I choose to become purposely naïve about the most critical things in my life.

Are you ready? Let's be naïve enough to believe what we want to see will happen. It could be something you want to see changed in your family, business, or community. Be encouraged by Nelson Mandela's words: "It always seems impossible until it's done."[96]

And the UNCOMMODiFiED always SEE IT FINISHED.

The innate ability to see it already achieved, to see it already done, already finished in your mind and heart is inspirational. The undeterred and undenied always visualize a situation improved and completed as though they are wearing special goggles.

I remember standing with Scott on the precipice of a dam in Zimbabwe, watching the water flow where once there was only dry land. He told me the story of the man who had the initial vision to build the dam. The man looked across the land, where the river ran through, and "saw" a dam that didn't exist. It didn't yet exist because there wasn't enough money or anyone to build it, and the civil engineer required to design it wasn't available. Soon his vision caught on, and others began to see it "done" as well. Eventually, money started flowing in, and one of the best civil engineers in the country offered to partner with them to build the dam. Scott saw it before it was, and then it was. That's the power of visualizing the dream before it is a reality.

Remember Tracy, who had a vision for a clinic and a place where children could be cared for without being made orphans? Children who otherwise would have been surrendered by their parents to orphanages could stay in their own homes with their families. She had a vision and could "see" it, done, finished. I remember standing with her, looking out at the open fields, as she "painted" a "picture" of what it could and would be. She saw it finished. And because she saw it already done, her vision enabled me and others to see it "done." That's the power of seeing the result as if it is already completed.

Or Julie, who sat with me under a tree and shared how she saw schools built and children educated. She SAW it finished, so I SAW it too. Together, we saw what was to come before it even existed. She and others were undeterred and undenied because it was already completed in their hearts and minds. And that's the power of seeing it already finished!

What about you? Are you a person of belief? Can you see what doesn't exist as though it did?

Uncommodify yourself and be undeterred and undenied. Don't let any force of nature deny you the fulfillment of your predestined future.

UNCAGE iT... NOW!

Are you undeterred? If so, explain how or why this is true of you.

If you are being pushed off course from something you are trying to achieve, ask yourself what you will do about that. What will be the benefits to yourself and others when you accomplish it?

How have you been denied or held back due to adversity or an adversary? What will you do about that?

How will you achieve what you want for yourself or others, for your community, your business, your friends, your family, or the world? How will achieving this goal change you and those around you?

Who is the most undeterred and undenied person you know?

Think about that person. Ruminate on their story, chew on their life, and think about why they are so undeterred and undenied.

Make a list of what you need to learn from them.

Review the twelve positive predispositions in this chapter. Then, identify two or three characteristics you need to strengthen and develop further. Write them here.

Think of ways you can strengthen them. What steps will you take to do so?

The Mystery and the Magic of the UN YET and the UN MET

Before you read this chapter, you may want to buy a magic wand and get ready to make some very practical magic.

7

THE UNCOMMODiFiED OUTLIERS I have had the privilege of encountering over my lifetime have taught me a magnificent lesson that I want to share with you as we get to the final stage of our roller-coaster ride towards our UNCOMMODiFiED destinies.

Mystery and some real magic reside in the unyet moments of our lives: the unyet experienced, unyet enjoyed, unyet explained, and unyet examined. Mystery and powerful magic reside in unmet people, unmet places, umet problems, and unmet possibilities. And the most potent magic brews and bubbles in your unyet story, which features the hero of your grand adventure: the "you" who you are becoming. So, get ready to turn the page and grab hold of what's next: your fantastic future. Get ready to meet the real hero of your story. Get ready to plunge your hand through the veil of the present moment. Get ready to pull your future into the present and find the mystery and the magic waiting for you there.

In this chapter, I want to investigate the unyet and the unmet in my life and yours. It's an exploration of the unyet, positive possibilities awaiting you and me and the possible unyet problems that may lurk around the corner.

"The real mystery and magic lives in the unyet and the unmet of our lives."

The prefix un means "not,"[97] at least not now or not so far. And when you think about it this way, even though something might not yet have happened, it doesn't mean it will not or cannot occur. It can still be. It may yet come. This is our UNYET. Of course, this is not a real word. We'll call it a "Tim word." I created it to describe something I desire or expect that has not yet happened, at least for the moment. But it may, it could, or it will. And it is also UNMET, because we have not met or encountered it yet.

So, here's my starting point for this final deep dive into this idea and its connection to becoming UNCOMMODiFiED — the real mystery and magic lives in the unyet and unmet of our lives. Little mystery remains in the past, whether past seasons or the most recent seconds of our life. Since we've already experienced it, we know it, so there is no longer any mystery left for us to discover, because it is done. And the present, well, it's what's happening right now. So the wait is over. The mystery is revealed.

So, here's the truth: I want to grab onto the provocative forces of mystery and magic, the enigmatic, enchanting future moments awaiting my creation, attention, and activation. I'm ready to unleash the mystery and the magic presently imprisoned in my unyet and unmet story. Unmet people and places, unyet and unmet positive possibilities, and unyet and unmet potential problems. Are you ready to unleash the mystery and the magic presently imprisoned in your unyet and your unmet?

Here's what I learned from my UNCOMMODiFiED gurus: I am the author, actor, playwright, and player in my story. I have consciously decided that I will be the one to write and tell it. Except, that has not always been the case. I have often given the pen, the paper, and the power to others. Sometimes, I have even felt like people occasionally stole those tools from me. Other times, I have willingly surrendered the pen, the paper, and the power to others. Regardless of how it happened and who did it, I now know I must OWN my story and my ability to WRITE and to TELL it. I do not have the ability to alter the already of my story. But I do have the power to shape the clay in my hands and form the unknown yet and the unmet. I can unlock the mystery and the magic of what is yet to come.

Of course, this idea applies not just to our personal life stories, but also to all the other stories we get to write: our family stories, business stories, charity stories, political stories and social action stories. It's not just a personal thing. Our businesses also have an already as well as an unyet and unmet. If you are involved in a charity, like I am, there's an already story of our charities and an unyet and unmet story still to be written. There are goals to be set, plans to be made, vision statements to be drafted, and declarations to be made.

What about you? Do you believe you're writing your own story? Do you fully claim the pen? Do you fully own the paper and the power? What does this mean to you? Do you like your answer? And, if you don't, what will you do about it?

I want to make this idea, which can seem a bit abstract, a bit more practical and personal by sharing the unfolding story of the one and only me. I am Tim Windsor, born on July 20, 1965, as Timothy Strome Windsor, and I will die on an unyet, unmet day and time. Between these two fixed timestamps is my story, most of which has already been told, already authored. Here are a few significant highlights from my already story from the year 1970, when I was five years old, to 1992, when I was 27.

August 1970 was the month my father left our family, the month he left me. That was a shitty plot twist in my story. In May 1974, my newly divorced mom had a nervous breakdown in public, hyperventilating as we rode a city bus. What a terrible experience for her and an embarrassing one for nine-year-old me. Fast forward to July 1981, when I had a powerful spiritual encounter that changed the direction of my story. On July 12, 1986, I married my best friend, beginning a new chapter of my life. My Papa, who was like a father to me, died in October of 1987. On July 6, 1989, I welcomed my firstborn, a daughter we named Melissa. What an incredible experience. In September 1990, I started my first marketing business that evolved into what I do today. And on December 19, 1992, my son Chris was born.

==All these events, whether tremendously positive or terrifyingly painful, came my way whether I wanted them to or not.== Over some of them, I had immense power, creative power. And over others, I felt like I had little to none. Whether predestined or fated by a god, gods or the god, or whether these events were random happenstance, all of these events have now passed. They are part of my "already" story, and that story is what it is. But that's not all it is. It's not the entire story. It's not all of who I am. While these past events and storylines define me in significant ways, they do not totally define me. And they don't automatically determine the following chapters I write. That gets to be my choice. And it's your choice, personally and professionally as well.

Let's discuss a more recent chapter of our collective story. Let's talk about COVID-19. For most of us, the year 2020 will go down as one of the most collectively challenging years. It was, after all, the pandemic year, the year of lockdown. It was the year of social distancing, the year of hiding our smiles and frowns behind masks. I went from traveling over 154 days in 2019 to sleeping, working, and relieving myself within a 24-step round-trip journey in my own home. What a change! Frankly, it sucked in so many ways. I don't know about you, but for me, it sucked. And yet, without minimizing the difficulty, you and I still retained a choice about how we authored, articulated, and acted out our story during this time. No one stole the power from us to decide how we would respond to the pandemic. We still got to choose, even had the responsibility to choose, the grand theme and narrative we wrote (and are writing) about that time. For some, the main plot was about the grief of it all. For others, like me, the main plot was the unexpected gifts that appeared during this time. Like my UNCOMMODiFiED Podcast that would not have been birthed if I wasn't stuck in my home office for almost two years.

"I GOT TO CHOOSE THE NARRATIVE: I HAVE THE PEN, THE PAPER, AND THE POWER."

Don't get me wrong, even though I chose to see 2020 as a gift, (I said as much in social media posts back in April 2020) some of my dialogue was dark and depressing and maybe even a little dangerous for myself and others. But I got to choose the narrative: I have the pen, the paper, and the power. And the mystery and magic live in the part of my story, the chapters unauthored and unacted. And it is true for you as well. We have the most control when we lean toward the future.

So here are five wisdom nuggets I received from my UNCOMMODiFiED sages that I use to ready myself for my unyet and unmet moments:

1. PERCEIVE THE PAST DIFFERENTLY.

Rewrite your stories of hardship and adversity. Rewrite your stories of when your father left you and your mother had a nervous breakdown on a bus. Actually, rewrite them as I did during my many therapy sessions over the years. I took my pen and paper and chose to see and write myself into these events again as an empowered, empathic observer of my father's and mother's personal pain, not a helpless victim of it for the rest of my life. Sure, there is no *undo* button in life. You can't undo things. You can't unsee things. You can't un-experience things (I know it's not a real word, but it's true). We can't go back and physically relive it differently. But here's the good news. We have a grand opportunity in front of us, as C.S. Lewis said, "You can't go back and change the beginning, but you can start where you are and change the ending."[98] And this is what I have done with the rather shitty plot twist of my father's choice to leave me and my family in 1970. After rewriting and reframing my view of that event as an empowered, empathic observer, I used that pain to propel me to become the kind of father to my children that I wanted him to be for me. I am humbled and proud to tell you that I have a fantastic friendship with my daughter Melissa, and my son Chris even asked me to be his best man at his wedding. Rescripting and reframing our experiences are the pathways to redeeming the past.

"SO, DON'T GAZE INTO THE REAR-VIEW MIRROR"

So, don't gaze into the rear-view mirror. Look through the windshield instead, and proactively and positively rewrite the painful parts of your already story so they can work FOR YOU and NOT AGAINST YOU in the future. Reinterpret and reimagine them as I have so that you can write a better future story.

2. BE A PROGNOSTICATOR.

Be a prophet and proactively predict your unyet and unmet. Start writing the future chapters now, don't just wait for them to happen to you. Ask yourself: What do I want to do? Who do I want to meet? Where do I want to go? Write your lists and turn them into scripts. Rehearse them and release them to the universe or to the great architect of the universe, if you believe there is one, and then prepare to realize them in your unyet and unmet story, as I did. As a teenager, I wrote a list of things I wanted to see and do, things that seemed improbable at that time. I didn't come from an affluent family. I didn't come from a place of privilege. Yet, I wrote a list that seemed impossible. I rehearsed the list and rescripted my life with it. And at the time I am writing this, only two things remain on that list that have not yet happened. But they will. I know they will because I "prophesied" them in advance.

3. PREP YOURSELF NOW.

Proactively prepare yourself for your unyet and unmet. Start working on yourself so you'll be ready to fully live your unyet and unmet possibilities. Do the hard work of readying yourself physically, mentally, intellectually, and psychologically. If being fully alive and healthy is part of your untold, unyet and unmet story, get yourself in shape so you can enjoy life and grab it by the horns. Take an online course, get some therapy, expose yourself to new ideas and develop your creativity like my wife did recently by taking classes to learn how to paint. Prepare yourself emotionally and spiritually for the future because those unyet and unmet moments are coming, and you won't fully live them unless you are ready.

4. BE PLIABLE.

Be open to the mystery and magic of it all. Be pliable and malleable. Prepare yourself to flex and change. Don't let your life's complicated storylines kill your spirit and will. **Be pliable and get ready to bend and lean into the mystery and magic of your unyet and unmet life.** Be prepared for all the coming plot twists. Welcome the surprise guests and unanticipated ups and downs that life (and others) throw your way. You will grow from them and develop muscles through the struggle. Like my friend Craig did when he was encouraged by his wife Marcia and family not to give up and get "paralyzed" after he became unemployed in his late 40s. Emboldened by their faith in him, he finally fulfilled his dream of creating a fantastic website called HistoryUnfurled.com. Here's how Craig's website was birthed: after taking a leave of absence due to stress, he returned to his job, where his boss made his return to work a nightmare. As a result, he left permanently. He resigned. And now he had time to write. Bottom-line: No asshole boss, means no public unfurling of Craig's love of history. Life has taught me that these kind of shitty plot twists may bring you more joy than you could ever have scripted for yourself. They have for Craig and his family.

5. And lastly, BE THE PLAYWRIGHT AND HERO OF YOUR OWN STORY.

Stop letting others write your story. Instead, focus on the future acts in your play. Make sure your present moment offers the best possible plot and narrative for you and for others. And be realistic: unforeseen and unwelcome plot twists will come. Shit's going to happen. Things you don't expect or want will happen. Other people will write you into their stories, and you may not like the character they craft for you. Just remember, never surrender your pen! Never surrender your paper and your power to others. Stop letting others write your story for you. Stop it right now. Take control of your narrative. I tell my clients, "Take control of your narrative in the market, write and tell your story to yourself and others, because if you don't, your competitors will write a different story of which you'll never be the hero."

Start to take control of your future story by asking this question:

> *How are you proactively predetermining, and preparing for your unyet and unmet story ... your future?*

Our lives are books of undisclosed lengths. Some of them are half-finished, and some are almost finished; we have no idea where we are in our story. Still, there are chapters to be discovered, words we have yet to write about who we are, what we are and who we must become. We have a pen, paper, and the power and opportunity to embrace the mystery and magic of our unyet and unmet story.

Consider the following: as the author and actor in your untold story, who is the hero of your current novel? And who will be the hero of your unyet and unmet personal and professional stories? The word *hero* comes from the Greek *heros*, which means "protector" or "defender."[99] As such, who has been your protector, defender, and hero in your story? And who will be the protector, defender, the hero in your unyet and unmet story?

Merriam-Webster's Dictionary also defines a hero as a "distinguished warrior."[100] So, who is the distinguished warrior in your already story, and who might it be in your unyet and unmet story?

Another definition of a hero is "one who shows great courage." Who is the courageous hero in your already story, the story that has already passed, and who will it be in your unyet and unmet story?

A hero is also the "principal character in a dramatic work." Who is the principal character in your story's drama, and who will it be in your unyet and unmet story?

Lastly, a hero can be defined as "a central figure in an event." Who is the central figure of your already story, and who will it be in your unyet and unmet story?

Here is my take on all this: YOU must be the hero in all these scenarios! The answer to all these questions is YOU. You are responsible for your story, your unyet and unmet story. You must be your protector and defender, your distinguished warrior. You must be the one who shows great courage and be the principal character in the dramatic work of your life. So, recognize yourself as the central figure in all your life's events. Just be willing to own the good, the bad, and the ugly.

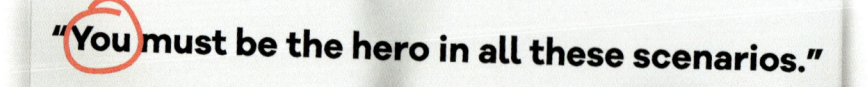

> "You must be the hero in all these scenarios."

American poet Casey Renee Kiser, in her poem entitled, *It's Getting Harder and Harder to Tell the Two of You Apart*, writes a brilliantly funny line: "I ain't nobody's sidekick. I am Batman. And Robin, minus the mask, plus the vagina."[101] Brilliant. And I echo her sentiment because, in my life, I am Batman. I am Robin minus the mask (except during COVID) plus a penis.

You might find a sidekick or two along the way, but you don't need one. Instead, you might just need to sidekick yourself in the ass occasionally and write a better story, a better unyet and unmet story.

So here's a question to consider:

Will you be the hero of your own life?

Or are you going to leave that role to someone else?

My UNCOMMODiFiED friends have taught me that being your own hero is simply about being a reliably devoted friend to yourself as you write your story. It is not about being superhuman or a superhero. It's about encouraging yourself to "show up" and fully feel the pleasure and even the pain encapsulated in each day. It's about choosing, when you fuck things up, to be kind and compassionate to yourself like you are to your best friends.

Like all great hero stories, we occasionally encounter an evil villain or two in the painful reality of our lives. And truthfully, as much as I don't want to admit it, **I have played both roles in my already story — hero and villain**. And I likely will in my unyet and unmet tale as well. And so will you. I call this dichotomy our hero-villain war, and it is just the unfortunate price of having a belly button. We are both villains and heroes because we are human. But you and I must stop being our own worst enemy and sabotaging our positive impact.

So, be the hero of your story. Write yourself into every scene without expecting others to notice your starring role, applaud for you or carry you on their shoulders for your heroic achievements. The most UNCOMMODiFiED people I know are comfortable being the "unsung" hero, the hero no one writes or sings about. They've taught me it's okay, even preferred and often necessary, to be the only one singing about your heroic exploits. Don't wait for others to sing your praise and call you a hero because if you do, you will never turn up to the right fight in your life. You'll miss your own story if you wait for someone else to sing your praises first.

So here's my best advice: **turn up your life's volume and impact today.** Live loud and quietly and be the unsung hero in the grand adventure of your unyet and unmet story. And don't forget to be your own reliably devoted friend along the way.

UNCAGE iT... NOW!

How accountable do you feel for the negative and challenging scenes of your already story and your reactions to them? Do you like your answer? And, if you don't, what will you do about it?

Rewrite a tale of adversity from your already story. What positive outcome could come to you if you do?

Consider your already story and look for times when you were your own hero and for times when you may have been your worst enemy. What can you learn from your memories of these experiences?

Look forward to your unyet and unmet story. How will you avoid being the villain in the future story?

How will you be more of your own hero in the future? How will you be your most reliably devoted friend this week? What positive outcomes do you foresee?

What does being the "unsung" hero of your untold story mean to you?

The Next Chapter... Our Unending Journey

AT THE END OF THE DAY ... if UNCOMMODiFiED is just a book you read, you missed the point. If it is just a chat with a whiskey-drinking, cigar and pipe-smoking kind of guy, even a rather uncomfortable chat at times that will not be good enough.

If it is just a candid conversation between you, me and my UNCOMMODiFiED mentors that stays on the pages of this book, that will not make any difference in your life. To be UNCOMMODiFiED, day-to-day, you must take the ideas, strategies, and examples you read and initiate positive and provocative actions that release the best version of yourself, the unique and amazing Homo sapien you are designed to be.

Nowhere in this book have I listed all the actions and attitudes of the UNCOMMODiFiED outliers I have discovered and documented over the past 30 years in one place for you to ponder. So here they are for you to review and ruminate on again.

Here's what we have discovered along the way:

The **UNCOMMODiFiED** ... See and slay six **UNTRUTHS** that put their uniqueness to sleep and induce a Commodity Coma ... **Embrace** their **UNIQUE Homo Sapien Self** ... **FALL FORWARD** ... **LEAN into LEARNING** ... **BACK UP, not DOWN** ... **SIT and STAY in the PAIN** ... remain **PURPOSELY NAÏVE** ... always **SEE IT FINISHED** ... crave the **Mystery** and **Magic** of the **UNYET** and the **UNMET** ... choose to **PERCEIVE the past differently** ... and **PREP themselves NOW** for their future.

The **UNCOMMODiFiED are** ... **UNFORGETTABLE** ... so **UNAFRAID** it's scary ... **UNCAGED** and **UNFETTERED** ... **UNMASKED** what-you-see-is-what-you-get kind of people ... **PROGNOSTICATORS** ... so **wonderfully UNASHAMED** that they'll make you blush ... comfortable making you and themselves "pants-way-too-tight" **UNCOMFORTABLE** ... almost **annoyingly UNRELENTING** ... **LONG HAULERS** ... so **UNFROZEN** they even warm the cold-hearted world around them ... wildly **UNBRIDLED** and **UNBRANDED** ... **UNCONDITIONALLY PERSONALLY ACCOUNTABLE** people who hold their own feet to the fire ... **TENACIOUSLY PATIENT** ... so radically **UNSELFISH** that they will inspire you to give until it heals ... always **UNUSUALLY PERPLEXED**; they spend most of their day scratching their head and questioning their last question ... **ENERGIZED BY FEAR** ... so **UTTERLY PERSUASIVE**; they can even get the naysayers to stop "naying." ... **UNSTOPPABLY PROACTIVE** action and nonaction superheroes ... terrible at playing hide-and-seek because they are **UNDENIABLY PRESENT** to everyone in the room ... **UNGUARDEDLY PASSIONATE**; they wear their heart and soul on their sleeve even when wearing a muscle shirt ... **PLIABLE** ... so **UNDERSTANDABLY PLAINSPOKEN** that they even come through loud and clear to the hard of hearing ... **AGGRESSIVE ANTAGONISTS** of the Status Quo ... **UNRESERVEDLY POSITIVE** people that even make "negative Nellies" see the bright side of life ... **UNABASHEDLY PLAYFUL** people who will never let "Jack" be a dull boy ... **ELASTIC** ... so **UNEQUIVOCALLY PRACTICAL** even Archimedes asks them to move the world for him ... Silver-tongued angels, **UNRIVALED "PAINTERS"** who can help you feel the heaven in your hell ... **UNDETERRED** and **UNDENIED** ... so **UNAPOLOGETICALLY PROVOCATIVE** you may find yourself thanking them for pissing you off enough to get you off your ass and into the arena ... and they are the **PLAYWRIGHT AND HERO OF THEIR OWN STORY.**

Here's my challenge to you; look back over these traits, and as you do, circle or highlight some of them and challenge yourself to UNCAGE their provocations in unique and practical ways within the very skinny part of the hourglass: the present moment where you live, love, laugh, lead, and learn.

As I type these final words to you, I am once again reminded that the journey, the roller coaster ride towards my UNCOMMODiFiED destiny, continues for me and hopefully, for you. Every day I challenge myself to discover and dissect more inspiring and instructional wisdom from the UNCOMMODiFiED outliers that I encounter and purposely engage.

So, here are two additional UNCOMMODiFiED traits I must reflect on and respond to. Over the past several years, I have recorded and released over 100 episodes of the UNCOMMODiFiED Podcast. Many of these episodes are "UNCORK Conversations" with people who live uniquely loud and quiet for the sake of others.

At the end of each of these conversational episodes, I always ask my guest to give us a window into their extraordinary world as they respond to this wonderous question, "When you are uncommodifying yourself, being and bringing your unique self into a room for the sake of others, what are you doing?" Over the

"I am once again reminded that the journey, the roller coaster ride towards my UNCOMMODiFiED destiny, continues for me and hopefully, for you."

years, all of their responses have inspired and incited my thinking and behaviour. In particular, two UNCOMMODiFiED provocations have demanded my attention and stimulated my action.

The first was born in the final moments of my UNCORK Conversation entitled "UNCOMMODIFYING ONE WORLD with ANOTHER" with Kris MacQueen. Kris is a Facilitator, Musician, Producer and my great friend. In response to that most wonderful question, he pulled this powerful provocation from the cosmos, "I believe in the power of the moment to be an impact … I can bring EARNEST HOPEFULNESS." That unexpected idea and insight shot through me like an arrow, through my mind, into my heart and lodged deep in my soul. As I reflected in the moment with Kris and in days after our recording session, I am even more convinced that Kris, me, and maybe even you (if you choose to) are most assuredly uncommodifying the space we share with other Homo sapiens as we articulate and activate our "EARNEST HOPEFULNESS" for them. When we "shout" our heartfelt belief and hope in others, it calls forth their faith and action and empowers them to do and be more. So, I have added this action and attitude to my ever-expanding list of the hallmarks of the UNCOMMODiFiED … **the UNCOMMODiFiED are EARNEST in their HOPEFULNESS for themselves and others.** Are you?

The other provocation that continues to demand my attention and stimulate my action was whispered into the ear of my heart at the end of an UNCORK Conversation entitled, "INTUITION: Get TUNED IN" with Erin Sikopoulos. Erin is a certified Gemstone Energy Medicine Practitioner, an Advanced Intuitive and a Licensed Massage Therapist. As we came to the moment of pregnant possibility, asking and answering once again that most wonderful question, "Erin when you are uncommodifying yourself, being and bringing your unique self into a room for the sake of others, what are you doing?" Her evocative revelation,

"I am diligently being an impeccable non-judgmental observer." Wow, and ouch! My immediate reflex — that's fucking hard to do, and what fantastic transformation could occur in me and in the one I am observing if I could activate this muscle and mission. What perspective could I discover that would allow me to see through someone else's "eyes" and "heart"? What would I see and learn as I humble myself and honour them through the willful suspension of my judgment? When we become an impeccable non-judgmental observer, full of graciousness, creative curiosity, and attentiveness to the world around us and the wanderer among us, we all find the transformation we seek. So, I have also now added this character trait to my ever-expanding list of the hallmarks of the UNCOMMODiFiED ... **the UNCOMMODiFiED are Impeccable Non-Judgmental Observers**. Are you?

BOTTOM-LINE and MY LINE IN THE SANDS OF TIME:

Being run of the mill. Being ordinary. Being mundane. Not an option for me. And, as you have discovered, these traits have not been options for the UNCOMMODiFiED provocateurs whom you have met on your journey with me. Along the way, you have encountered some of the people who have caught my attention over the years in both mystical and magical ways. They are inspiringly different, positively provocative, utterly unique, and outstanding in their approaches to possibilities and problems, in how they lead and work, and in how they live their lives. They stand apart in the best, most positive ways, in ways that can be transformational for all of us. They are beckoning all of us to NOT surrender our uniqueness and NOT give into homogeneity because they know that this surrender will ultimately and utterly infuse our veins with the anesthetizing power of sameness.

UNCAGE iT... NOW!

What extraordinary and UNCOMMODiFiED action must you take today to break the evil spell of sameness?

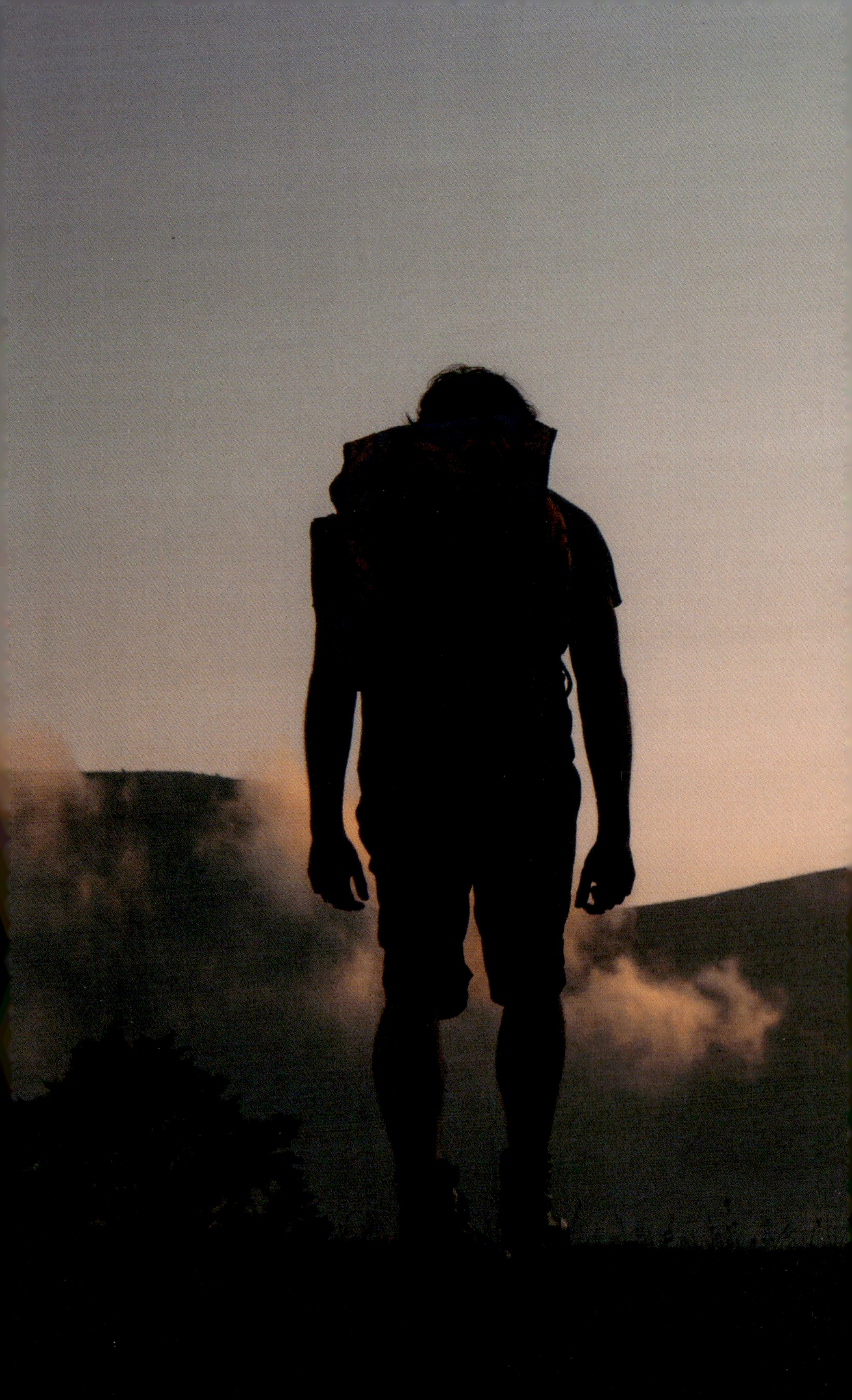

ENDNOTES

1 National Human Genome Research Institute (NHGRI) website: genome.gov
2 The Healthy @Reader's Digest website: thehealthy.com
3 National Library of Medicine website: ncbi.nlm.nih.gov
4 Hearing Health Foundation website: hearinghealthfoundation.org
5 brainyquote.com/quotes/georg_c_lichtenberg_404045
6 goodreads.com/quotes/119070-a-half-truth-is-the-most-cowardly-of-lies
7 quotefancy.com/quote/857458/Mahatma-Gandhi-Even-a-little-untruth-destroys-a-man-as-a-drop-of-poison-ruins-milk
8 founders.archives.gov/documents/Jefferson/03-05-02-0478
9 STUDY - Hasher, Lynn; Goldstein, David; Toppino, Thomas (1977). "Frequency and the conference of referential validity" (PDF). Journal of Verbal Learning and Verbal Behavior. 16 (1): 107–112. doi:10.1016/S0022-5371(77)80012-1. Archived from the original on 2016-05-15.
10 en.wikipedia.org/wiki/Illusory_truth_effect. Dreyfuss, Emily (February 11, 2017). "Want to Make a Lie Seem True? Say It Again. And Again. And Again". Wired. Archived from the original on 6 May 2021. Retrieved 31 October 2017.
11 bible.com JAMES 1-23 NLT
12 en.wikipedia.org/wiki/Illusory_truth_effect. Dreyfuss, Emily (February 11, 2017). "Want to Make a Lie Seem True? Say It Again. And Again. And Again". Wired. Archived from the original on 6 May 2021. Retrieved 31 October 2017.
13 goodreads.com/quotes/372803-that-which-hurts-also-instructs
14 youtube.com/watch?v=ziOG_GHNVq0&list=PL1E60F8F526CDC2B3
15 youtube.com/watch?v=LhQGzeiYS_Q
16 (Source: Aion (1951). CW 9, Part II: P.14)
17 azlyrics.com/lyrics/brucecockburn/loversinadangeroustime.html
18 https://en.wikipedia.org/wiki/Golden_Rule
19 everydayhealth.com/cognitive-dissonance/
20 languages.oup.com/
21 https://www.dictionary.com/browse/unrelenting
22 https://www.britannica.com/biography/Olaf-Engelbrektsson
23 frozen.fandom.com/wiki/Some_People_Are_Worth_Melting_For
24 themacqueens.ca/music
25 https://www.quotespedia.org/authors/a/anita-krizzan/when-it-hurts-observe-life-is-trying-to-teach-you-something-anita-krizzan/
26 https://www.idiva.com/entertainment/hollywood/7-lessons-i-learnt-from-disneys-frozen/33752
27 americanrhetoric.com/speeches/mlkivebeentothemountaintop.htm
28 powerquotations.com/quote/the-human-being-who-lives
29 https://www.vocabulary.com/dictionary/ennoble
30 bible.com Genesis 2:4-3:24 NLT
31 theguardian.com/science/2018/mar/14/best-stephen-hawking-quotes-quotations
32 brainyquote.com/quotes/albert_einstein_174001
33 theglobeandmail.com/arts/art-and-architecture/biographer-walter-isaacson-explains-what-made-leonardo-da-vinci-a-genius/article37176982/
34 quotefancy.com/quote/228181/Edward-R-Murrow-To-be-persuasive-we-must-be-believable-to-be-believable-we-must-be
35 philosiblog.com/2014/02/22/luck-is-what-happens-when-preparation-meets-opportunity/
36 https://www.lindau-nobel.org/chance-favors-the-prepared-mind/
37 https://www.azquotes.com/author/2886-Winston_Churchill/tag/planning
38 https://dictionary.cambridge.org/dictionary/english/there-s-no-rest-for-the-wicked
39 tinybuddha.com/wisdom-quotes
40 https://en.wikipedia.org/wiki/Matthew_6:27
41 procrastinus.com/procrastination/the-definition-of-procrastination/
42 merriam-webster.com/thesaurus/procrastinate
43 https://neuroleadership.com/your-brain-at-work/the-myth-of-multitasking
44 psychologytoday.com/ca/blog/creativity-without-borders/201405/the-myth-of-multitasking
45 en.wiktionary.org/wiki/passion
46 thesaurus.com/browse/passion
47 en.wiktionary.org/wiki/enthusiasm
48 quotefancy.com
49 dictionary.com/browse/may

50 dictionary.com/browse/be
51 Getting to Maybe: How the world is changed - by Westley, Zimmerman and Patton - 2006
52 en.wikipedia.org/wiki/Pollyanna
53 https://adventurenannies.com/blog/mr-rogers-quotes/
54 The saying first appeared in James Howell's Proverbs in 1659
55 https://www.goodreads.com/quotes/99144-man-s-maturity-to-have-regained-the-seriousness-that-he-had
56 https://psychcentral.com/blog/the-importance-of-play-for-adults
57 https://www.shondaland.com/live/body/a36123122/adults-need-playtime-as-much-as-kids/
58 https://www.ncbi.nlm.nih.gov/pmc/articles/PMC5646690/
59 https://psychcentral.com/blog/the-importance-of-play-for-adults
60 https://www.goodreads.com/quotes/22847-the-creation-of-something-new-is-not-accomplished-by-the
61 https://usplaycoalition.org/play-the-fountain-of-youth-the-role-of-play-in-adult-neurogenesis
62 https://usplaycoalition.org/play-the-fountain-of-youth-the-role-of-play-in-adult-neurogenesis
63 https://usplaycoalition.org/play-the-fountain-of-youth-the-role-of-play-in-adult-neurogenesis
64 https://www.goodreads.com/quotes/413462-we-don-t-stop-playing-because-we-grow-old-we-grow
65 https://www.chesterton.org/heaven-is-a-playground/%20-%20from%20the%20essay%20%E2%80%9COxford%20from%20Without%E2%80%9D%20in%20the%201908%20book,%C2%A0All%20Things%20Considered.
66 quotefancy.com/quote/19939/Albert-Einstein-In-theory-theory-and-practice-are-the-same-In-practice-they-are-not
67 brainyquote.com/quotes/oliver_wendell_holmes_sr_152682
68 https://www.collinsdictionary.com/dictionary/english/practical
69 https://en.wiktionary.org/wiki/practicus
70 https://www.poetryfoundation.org/poems/56966/speech-all-the-worlds-a-stage
71 brainyquote.com/quotes/samuel_smiles_126461
72 plainlanguage.gov
73 thesaurus.com/browse/plainspoken
74 youtube.com/watch?v=vP4iY1TtS3s
75 masterclass.com/articles/metaphor-similie-and-analogy-differences-and-similarities
76 scienceworld.ca/stories/metaphors-and-your-brain/
77 en.wiktionary.org/wiki/life_is_like_a_box_of_chocolates
78 en.wikipedia.org/wiki/Icarus
79 https://www.encyclopedia.com/humanities/dictionaries-thesauruses-pictures-and-press-releases/provocative
80 bible.com Hebrews 10-24 NLT
81 https://www.merriam-webster.com/thesaurus/provocative
82 dictionary.com/browse/evocator
83 https://www.merriam-webster.com/dictionary/undeterred
84 https://www.goodreads.com/quotes/5233279-it-s-hard-to-beat-a-person-who-never-gives-up
85 en.wikipedia.org/wiki/Pareto_principle
86 brainyquote.com/quotes/archimedes_101761
87 huffpost.com/entry/21-famous-failures-who-refused-to-give-up_b_57da2245e4b04fa361d991ba
88 merriam-webster.com/dictionary/tenacious
89 en.wiktionary.org/wiki/status_quo
90 https://www.thelifecoach.com/henry-fords-secrets-success/
91 brainyquote.com/quotes/thomas_a_edison_149049
92 forbes.com/quotes/8999/
93 brainyquote.com/quotes/albert_einstein_106192
94 en.wikipedia.org/wiki/Antifragility
95 en.wikipedia.org/wiki/Antifragility
96 brainyquote.com/quotes/nelson_mandela_378967
97 dictionary.com/browse/un
98 https://quotefancy.com/quote/781638/C-S-Lewis-You-can-t-go-back-and-change-the-beginning-but- you-can-start-where-you-are-and
99 en.wiktionary.org/wiki/hero
100 merriam-webster.com/dictionary/hero
101 goodreads.com/quotes/10047139-i-ain-t-nobody-s-sidekick-i-am-batman-and-robin-minus

PHOTO CREDITS

NODS, WINKS & KUDOS ...
Aidan Hennebry

SO WHAT IS THIS BOOK ABOUT? ...
Robynne Hu courtesy of Unsplash.com
https://unsplash.com/photos/HOrhCnQsxnQ

CHAPTER 1 ...
Itai Aarons courtesy of Unsplash.com
https://unsplash.com/photos/THcBzXzG2tA

CHAPTER 1 ... (Tim Windsor)
Aidan Hennebry

CHAPTER 2 ...
Danny Lines courtesy of Unsplash.com
https://unsplash.com/photos/QlrHRcDj4QE

CHAPTER 3 ...
Nathan Dumlao courtesy of Unsplash.com
https://unsplash.com/photos/pUThiwbUn8I

CHAPTER 3 ... (Final image)
Jason Blackeye courtesy of Unsplash.com
https://unsplash.com/photos/iMJZ7wzLxYU

CHAPTER 4 ...
Andriy Popov courtesy of 123RF.com

CHAPTER 4 ... (Final image)
Stars Studio courtesy of 123RF.com

CHAPTER 5 ...
Mohamed Nohassi courtesy of Unsplash.com
https://unsplash.com/photos/odxB5oIG_iA

CHAPTER 5 ... (Paper Note)
Kelly Sikkema courtesy of Unsplash.com
https://unsplash.com/photos/mdADGzyXCVE

CHATPER 5 ... (Fire)
Brady Rogers courtesy of Unsplash.com
https://unsplash.com/photos/AAB4iERjvco

CHAPTER 5 ... (People on Rock)
Joshua Earle courtesy of Unsplash.com

CHAPTER 6 ...
Joshua Earle courtesy of Unsplash.com
https://unsplash.com/photos/9idqIGrLuTE

CHAPTER 7 ...
Rhett Wesley courtesy of Unsplash.com
https://unsplash.com/photos/NQexDDK9P9w

THE LAST CHAPTER ...
Khamkéo Vilaysing courtesy of Unsplash.com
https://unsplash.com/photos/AMQEB4-uG9k

THE LAST CHAPTER ... (Final image)
Rollf Images courtesy of 123RF.com

FINAL IMAGE ...
Mukuko Studio courtesy of Unsplash.com
https://unsplash.com/photos/tPKQwYHy8q4

UNCAGE iT NOW IMAGE ...
Gelphi courtesy of 123RF.com